Sharing the Gospel with Our Lives

Sharing the Gospel with Our Lives

A Relational Approach to Catholic Youth Ministry

BOB RICE

Our Sunday Visitor
Huntington, Indiana

Nihil Obstat
Msgr. Michael Heintz, Ph.D.
Censor Librorum
Imprimatur
✠ Kevin C. Rhoades
Bishop of Fort Wayne-South Bend
June 15, 2024

The *Nihil Obstat* and *Imprimatur* are official declarations that a book is free from doctrinal or moral error. It is not implied that those who have granted the *Nihil Obstat* and *Imprimatur* agree with the contents, opinions, or statements expressed.

29 28 27 26 25 24   1 2 3 4 5 6 7 8 9

Our Sunday Visitor Publishing Division
Our Sunday Visitor, Inc.
200 Noll Plaza
Huntington, IN 46750
www.osv.com
1-800-348-2440

ISBN: 978-1-63966-149-7 (Inventory No. T2859)
1. RELIGION—Christian Ministry—Youth.
2. RELIGION—Christian Education—Children & Youth.
3. RELIGION—Christianity—Catholic.
eISBN: 978-1-63966-150-3
LCCN: 2024942422

Cover design: Tyler Ottinger
Interior design: Amanda Falk
Cover art: Adobe Stock

PRINTED IN THE UNITED STATES OF AMERICA

To Fr. Francis Dubois and the amazing volunteers and teenagers I had the blessing to minister with at the Church of St. Ambrose in Latham, New York

Contents

Foreword

Who, me?!?

"I could never be a youth minister."

Those were the seven words I thought would get me off the hook. It was the second semester of my senior year in college. I already had a job — nay, a *career* — lined up that would actually pay me enough to eat. Graduation was in sight. All that was left was to pack up my stuff, move into my new apartment, and find a nearby Catholic parish where I could disappear into the ether every Sunday like a dutiful son from a big Catholic family.

That's when the phone in my dorm room rang, and my life began to quickly unravel. These were the days before caller ID, when life was far more thrilling (not to mention risky) because every incoming call was an unknown adventure. As I answered, I quickly recognized the voice on the other end; it was the pastor of my home parish who was instrumental in my own conversion at sixteen years old. After a few moments of awkward small talk where I tried to sound as holy and pious as possible, he said,

"Hey, there's something I want you to pray about ..."

Pause. I hate when priests do that. Ugh.

"What's that, Father?"

"I want you to pray about coming back and being my youth minister," he replied.

Now, to be clear, I owed a great deal both to him and to my youth minister, who came along at a critical juncture in my adolescent life. They both saw something in me that I hadn't seen in myself, and they spoke truth with conviction and mercy into my prideful, shallow, egocentric, sixteen-year-old life. So I had a soft spot for the youth ministry program and for kids like me. Regardless, I was really excited about the career path I had lined up, and I had *no* plans of going into full-time ministry. I hadn't even majored in theology! That's when it hit me: the perfect "Get out of hell ministry-free" card.

"Father, I'm flattered," I responded, "but I'm not a theologian."

Boom. Game. Set. Match. There's no way he was prepared for that one. Father was assuredly outmatched by my stunningly obvious declaration. He brought a knife to a gunfight. Meanwhile, I had secured my "out" while still preserving our relationship.

His response, however, quickly turned my own answer against me, revealing that I was holding a mere squirt gun in this fight.

"Mark, I can teach someone who loves teens the theology ... but I can't teach a theologian to love my teenagers."

At that moment, heaven and earth collided within me. My heart was conflicted yet fulfilled. My mind was flooded with peace, my soul overflowing with conviction. I assured Father I would pray as I hung up the phone, but I already knew my answer. The Holy Spirit whispered to me as I sat on my horrible, ten-dollar dorm room couch, "Mark, *this is what I have prepared you for.*"

I told the Lord — and later, Father — that I'd serve one year in youth ministry. At the time of this writing, I am happily entering into my twenty-eighth, and it's been the best decision of my life.

Yes, YOU!!

I'm not exactly sure how you came to have this book in your hands, but I am very glad that you do. Whether you are brand-new to the mission of youth ministry, a seasoned vet, a master catechist, or an adult with a full-time job/family/responsibilities who sees a need and just wants to do "something" for the teens of your parish and community, I want to thank you. Sincerely, from the bottom of my heart, thank you for answering the call. If I had not had adults who cared enough to walk with me in high school, not only would I not be Catholic today, I doubt I'd even be alive.

I've known Deacon Bob Rice for over twenty-five years and have served beside him in numerous capacities at countless events. He's a trusted and dear friend of mine, and there is a great deal I could tell you about him, but you'll undoubtedly glean much of what I'd share on the pages that follow. Two things I do want to mention, though, are that Bob is wonderfully insane and deeply sincere. Yes, he's insane. He's funny and unpredictable yet incredibly down-to-earth. He has a way of sharing truth that is attractive and not off-putting, which is why he was such a tremendous parish youth minister and master teacher. Even more inviting, however, is Bob's abiding sincerity. When you sit and talk with him — whether about the sacraments or Star Wars — there is no duplicity, no guile, no hidden agenda. Bob knows and loves the Lord, and his sole mission is to see that everyone else does, too.

On the pages that follow, you will be given a true gift: essential insights into teenage culture, the challenges and struggles teens face, the needs they have, and the call of us all to engage. Bob offers practical advice stemming from real-life experience in the youth ministry trenches — not theoretical, fanciful ideas from an academic hidden away, afraid to engage.

Drawing from Sacred Scripture, the *Catechism of the Catholic Church*, and masterful wisdom of the saints and modern popes, this book will present you with both the challenge and the solution for our young Church. Now, to be clear, there will be some moments when you might feel uncomfortable or overwhelmed; or the enemy may even come and whisper to you that you cannot do this, but nothing could be further from the truth. You can do "*all things* through [Christ] who strengthens [you]" (Phil 4:13, emphasis added).

Youth ministry — true youth ministry, no youth "programming" — requires time, patience, mercy, more patience, and consistency on the part of the adult accompanying the youth. Take to heart the lessons and thoughts offered within this book, devote yourself to prayer (daily), and watch miracles happen within your own parish and community.

The greatest commodity you have to share is your time, and the greatest gift, your love for the Lord and his people. Give the Holy Spirit permission to move in new ways in your life and ministry — and hold on tight. Great things are going to happen in time. I'm grateful to Deacon Bob for writing this resource, and I'm grateful to you for being bold (and insane) enough to say yes to this calling.

Now, say a prayer before you turn this page. A new adventure awaits.

All for her son,
Mark Hart
CIO, Life Teen International
June 2024

1
The Second Mile

Our story begins, like any good story, with a wizard.

Not a wizened old wizard, such as Gandalf from *The Lord of the Rings*. A teenage wizard. And no, he didn't have round glasses and a scar on his head.

His skin was as pale as a corpse. His lips were painted black. I believe he had on dark eyeliner as well. He wore a black mesh shirt (with nothing underneath it), and on his neck was a spiked dog collar. He was the "chief wizard" of a group of teens who were involved in the occult at the local public high school.

I had been told that he might show up that night. One of my teens was in an art class with him, and he had started making fun of her over a retreat T-shirt she was wearing. He mentioned something about her being a hypocrite, like all her Catholic friends. She asked if he ever hung out with Catholics. When he said no, she turned the tables on him and said that *he* was the hypocrite for judging people he's never met. She said if he ever wanted to find out what Catholics are really like, there was a youth group meeting every Sunday at 6:00 p.m., and he was welcome to come.

To her shock, he replied, "I'll see you there."

I pulled my volunteers together before the meeting, letting them know there might be someone unusual visiting tonight, and to treat him like any other teen. So, when he came in, none of us acted shocked, none commented about the dog collar. "My name is Bob," I said, extending my hand.

He started at it, then looked up at me. "Jeremy," he said, loosely shaking my hand.

Jeremy stood in the back. He didn't say much. He didn't get involved in the activities of the night. I expected him to duck out in the middle of the meeting, but he stayed to the very end.

To my (and everyone else's) surprise, he came back the next week. And the next. I started having conversations with him, as did other adults and teens in the group. We had a retreat coming up and invited him to go on it. He did!

Our retreats were very focused on proclaiming the Gospel message and encouraging teenagers to "own" their faith, giving them a chance to publicly do so at an open mic on Saturday night. After a number of teens shared how they had encountered Jesus in a new way that weekend, Jeremy stood up. You could hear a pin drop as he approached the microphone. A female volunteer who sat next to me grabbed my arm and dug her nails into my skin. *This was it.*

"I thought going on this retreat would suck," Jeremy said. "But actually ..."

We all held our breath.

"It didn't suck as bad as I thought it would." He walked back to his seat.

The volunteer looked at me, confused. I shrugged. "Baby steps," I whispered.

But he kept coming back. His friends in the occult started making fun of him because of it, and that's when he realized that *they* were the hypocrites, while the people at church genuinely seemed to like him just for who he was. A year later, Jeremy went through RCIA and entered the Catholic Church. That girl he made fun of? He asked her to be his godmother.

He is one of many whose lives were changed because they encountered Jesus through the relationships that we built with them. I *believe* in youth ministry and the power it has to transform lives. It changed mine when I was a teenager. In my decades of parish work and travels, I've seen it change the lives of hundreds, if not thousands of teenagers.

What Is Youth Ministry, Anyway?

Youth ministry is a nebulous term for doing ministry for and with young people that can happen in many different settings. Some of the more obvious are parish youth ministry, Catholic junior high and high schools, OCIA for teenagers, or confirmation preparation. There are also many ministry opportunities with youths in sports leagues, leadership programs, camp ministries, Boy Scouts/Girl Scouts/Trail Life groups, military bases, pregnancy centers, juvenile detention centers, homeless shelters, and foster homes, just to name a few. All of these come under the umbrella of "youth ministry."

People often think of youth ministry as a "youth group," which they assume is a social environment of pizza and dodgeball. If that is all that we offer to teens then, yes, that isn't very effective. But what if, along with pizza and dodgeball (because both are awesome), that "group" provides an opportunity to get to know caring adults and peers who take their relationship with Jesus seriously? What if it is a place where the Good News is proclaimed in a relevant way? What if it becomes a place where teenagers feel welcomed and loved, where they can ask questions without condemnation? Such "groups" can be powerful places of conversion in young people's lives.

Ideally, a parish or faith community provides multiple access points that cater to the divergent ages, environments, and stages of faith among teenagers. Examples can include a weekly, high-energy meeting focused on building community and a basic proclamation of the Gospel, smaller group Bible or *Catechism* studies to grow deeper in the Faith, weekend retreats, social activities, sports, mission trips, camping experiences, service opportunities, sacramental celebrations, leadership training, small group mentoring, and the like. All these activities should have as their eventual goal to immerse teens in (not isolate them from) the wider faith community.

I've always appreciated this description of youth ministry from the US bishops' 1976 document, *A Vision of Youth Ministry*: "Youth ministry is the response of the Christian community to the needs of young people, and the sharing of the unique gifts of youth with the larger community." The reciprocal dynamic of this definition is important. Youth ministry begins when the Christian community recognizes the painful divide that exists between youths and adults and becomes determined to bridge the gap. They realize that young people need the wisdom, experience, and maturity (among other things) that adults can provide, and that adults need the gifts the young have to offer, such as vitality, creativity, and enthusiasm.

Though the goal is to be a vibrant faith community of adults and youths, it is the responsibility of adults (after all, we are supposed to have wisdom, right?) to take the initiative and reach out to teens. In Latin, the word *minister* comes from the word *minus* (less), meaning that we have to become "less than" the other in order to serve and help them. If that surprises you, realize that is it no "less" than what Jesus did for us: "Who, though he was in the form of God, / did not regard equality with God something to be grasped. / Rather, he emptied himself, / taking the form of a slave, / coming in human likeness; / and found human in appearance, / he humbled himself, / becoming obedient to death, / even death on a cross" (Phil 2:6–8).

Put another way, youth ministry happens when adults (like you) humble themselves to love and serve young people, just as Jesus did.

The Need for Youth Ministry

Youth ministry has been getting a bad rap lately. One statement that I frequently hear is "If Catholic parents did their job and raised their kids in the Faith, we wouldn't need youth ministry." That is simply not true. Yes, those in ministry with teens frequently need to evangelize teenagers who "should" have learned about the Faith at home. But I've also seen teenagers from strong Catholic families who were tremendously blessed by the ministry that we did with them.

YOUTH MINISTRY HAPPENS WHEN ADULTS (LIKE YOU) HUMBLE THEMSELVES TO LOVE AND SERVE YOUNG PEOPLE, JUST AS JESUS DID.

Even if a family does all the right things, it is incredibly difficult to be a teenage disciple of Jesus Christ in this culture. They need all the help that they can get! I'd like to think of myself as a pretty devoted Catholic dad, but even I can't offer to my teens the kinds of things that a good Catholic youth ministry program can: a group of like-minded peers to hang out with, caring adults who reflect different vocations and paths to holiness, messages that speak directly to challenging cultural issues, and opportunities to serve others and share their faith with their friends (just to name a few).

I've also heard it said that if the family isn't faithful, their teens won't be faithful. This will likely be true, *unless we do something about it.* Saint Paul wrote: "For I am not ashamed of the gospel. It is the power of God for the salvation of everyone who believes" (Rom 1:16). I'm not saying that it isn't more of a challenge for a teen to be faithful if their family is not. I'm saying that the Holy Spirit has overcome more difficult obstacles than that. If our faith lives were solely dependent on our genealogy, then few of us would be faithful Catholics.

Teens from faithful Catholic families need a community of loving adults and peers to accompany them on the turbulent road of adolescence to discover God's call in their life. What does a teen from an atheistic family need? The exact same thing.

"Doesn't everyone need that?" you may ask. Yes, but — and this is important — *teenagers need it more.* Adolescence is a time of transitions, decisions, and directions that often determine the entire trajectory of one's life. The physical, emotional, cognitive, and even spiritual changes that occur during the years of adolescence provide a unique moment for the Gospel message to take root in their life. If we miss that moment, we might lose that person. Statistics over the past decades have shown that large numbers of young people have left the Church and have not come back (as previous generations assumed they would).

Ministry That Makes a Difference

When adults lament the lack of youth participation in their parish, sometimes I ask, "Why?" They look at me as if I had two heads. "Because if youths stop coming, our parishes will close!" they exclaim. That's a bit selfish, isn't it?

The better reason for doing youth ministry comes from Scripture. "For the love of Christ impels us, once we have come to the conviction that one died for all; therefore, all have died. He indeed died for all, so that those who live might no longer live for themselves but for him who for their sake died and was raised" (2 Cor 5:14–15). Our motivation for ministry is what we celebrate during the Easter Triduum: Jesus Christ, through his death and resurrection, offers us all new life with him. Saint Paul goes on to write, "So whoever is in Christ is a new creation: the old things have passed away; behold, new things have come" (2 Cor 5:17). This is the goal, to be a "new creation" in the life of grace.

If we believe the words of Jesus that he is "the way and the truth and the life" (Jn 14:6), then we must also acknowledge that without Jesus we are lost, deceived, and dead. This is the tragic situation of many teenagers (and adults) today. The stakes could not be higher. Jesus didn't die on a cross to help us be nicer people. Through his cross and resurrection, he obliterated death and sin, and now offers new life for those who are willing to follow him.

Adolescence is a time of making decisions, and the most important decision a person can make is whether to believe or reject the Gospel. This goes beyond simply believing that there *is* a God, for "even the demons believe that and tremble" (Jas 2:19). It is about accepting his mercy, surrendering our will, and offering our lives to the One who gave his life for us.

There are five things every teenager has a right to know:

1. There is a God who is passionately in love with you;
2. There is a mercy greater than any sin that you can ever commit;
3. There is a truth more satisfying than any lie that you can ever believe;
4. There is no greater adventure than being a disciple of Jesus Christ; and
5. There is no place you are more greatly needed than in his Church.

We can't just *say* this to them. We have to *share* this with them. The question is, how?

Well, how did Jesus do it? That is the focus of this book:

to see how Jesus — who "became flesh and made his dwelling among us" (Jn 1:14) — did ministry with others and apply those principles to the ministry that we do with teenagers.

The Not-So-Extra Mile

Jesus famously said, "Should anyone press you into service for one mile, go with him for two miles" (Mt 5:41). It is easy to miss how shocking that command would sound in the ears of a first-century Jew. One of the many humiliating laws that Rome enacted on its conquered people was that Roman soldiers could force them into service for one mile. You could be minding your own business or busy at work when a Roman soldier would yell for your attention and make you carry his gear up to a mile. After a mile, you could put it down and go back as he picked a new person to carry it the next mile.

"Go with him for two miles." Can you imagine the shock of a Roman soldier who informed a Jew that he could go back and instead was told, "Actually, I'm happy to go another mile with you." The attitude of the Roman toward the Jew in that second mile would be radically different than the first. He might even ask, "Why?" Then the other might say, "Well, there is this guy named Jesus ..."

Relational ministry is the "extra mile" in ministry with youths. Or perhaps it would be more accurate to call it the "not-so-extra mile." Today, when you hear about someone going the extra mile, it means they went above and beyond what they were supposed to do. But for followers of Jesus, the extra mile isn't "extra" at all. It is required. It is what sets us apart as disciples of Jesus. And it is where the real ministry happens.

Some people confuse "relational ministry" with being friendly to teens who show up at church events, just as some confuse "evangelization" with being nice. Obviously, we should be nice to the teens who come to our confirmation classes or youth groups.

That's the first mile. The things we do beyond the requirements of the program are the second. Things like cheering them on at sporting events, attending their band concerts, reading a book or listening to music that they are excited about, visiting them if they are in the hospital, showing up at a funeral for one of their relatives, tutoring them in a subject that you are good at, sending them a care package at college … the list can go on and on.

Another way of understanding relational ministry is sharing the Faith through friendship. These kinds of friendships are unusual. Most of our friendships happen because of convenience (they happen to live on your block, they went to your school, they are colleagues at work) or commonality (you root for the same team, you have similar political beliefs, you share the same faith). The teenagers you minister with might not be at any of the places you would normally be or have many interests in common. Maybe they go to your church. *Maybe.*

Since they likely won't go where you are, you go to them. Since there might not be much in common, you search for commonalities, even starting to care about things they care about just because it is an opportunity to care about them. The unusual nature of this kind of friendship makes it no less genuine than others. They are not unnatural; they are *supernatural.* This is what Jesus did in the Incarnation. He came to us. He *became* us. And he said, "You are my friends if you do what I command you" (Jn 15:14). Relational ministry follows the model of Christ. We build friendships with teenagers so they can become friends with Jesus.

We can't shy away from the commitment that it takes to do this kind of ministry with teenagers. Those of you who are already involved know the sacrifice that it takes. It isn't just a bigger time commitment, but a bigger "heart" commitment. It means rejoicing when they rejoice, mourning when they mourn. Young people will exceed your wildest hopes and fall short of

RELATIONAL MINISTRY FOLLOWS THE MODEL OF CHRIST. WE BUILD FRIENDSHIPS WITH TEENAGERS SO THEY CAN BECOME FRIENDS WITH JESUS.

your most basic expectations, sometimes doing both in one weekend. They will fill you with incredible joy. They will break your heart. Young people are on a roller coaster where their highs are very high, and their lows are very low. Some live with burdens that you can't imagine. They will inspire you. They will help you see the world in a different way. They will make you question your faith. They will draw you closer to God.

Who, Me?

Jesus said to his disciples, "The harvest is abundant but the laborers are few; so ask the master of the harvest to send out laborers for his harvest" (Mt 9:37–38). This is a dangerous prayer. We can rightly fear that, if we pray for the Lord to send others into the harvest, he might send us instead.

Spoiler alert: *He does.*

The lives of teenagers will be changed by the relationships that you build with them. I've seen a *lot* of youth ministry programs over the years. I've seen youth groups that had the lights and sounds of a rock concert with hundreds of kids in attendance. I've been in living rooms with a mom who was a part-time youth minister at the parish (insert laughter here; there is no such thing as "part-time" ministry) with nine teenagers, and two of them were her kids. Either approach can work, and either approach can fail.

Success in youth ministry isn't about the quantity of teens but the quality of relationships. Relationships with *who*? With *you.* Relationships that lead them closer to Christ. The harvest is plenty. Fruit that isn't harvested goes to waste. Tragically, every person who says, "Not me," adds a few more lives that won't be transformed by the Gospel.

Before you feel overwhelmed by expectations, when I say, "you," I don't mean *just* you. Ideally, you are one of a number of holy friendships that a teenager will have with caring adults that will model for them the joyful life of being a disciple of Jesus Christ in the Catholic Church. We go forth as a loving community of faith. The larger that community, the more teenagers are welcomed into it, the more lives are changed, the more God is glorified.

It is that simple. It's just not that easy. So that's why I wrote this book.

Sharing the Gospel with Our Lives

There is a lot to say about ministry with youths. If I tried to put it into one book, it would be very thick and — can we be honest? — you wouldn't read it. Of the many descriptors I would use for those I've met in youth ministry, "readers" doesn't quite float to the top (no offense).

This book is focused on the most essential "skill" needed for those who do ministry with Catholic teenagers: sharing the Faith through friendship. This can be applied to any ministry environment with teens, whether it be in high school or junior high, parish or campus, weeklong camp or day retreat, or mandatory confirmation preparation or volunteer service project.

The first part of this book is a Bible study. We will look at the fourth chapter of John to examine how Jesus transformed the life of the woman at the well (with an added bonus of the road to Emmaus). The second part will look at how we can do the same with teenagers through our relationships with them.

The story of salvation history is filled with God using unqualified and unlikely people to do extraordinary things for his glory (for example, *me*). I continually marvel that God not only invites us to be a part of his kingdom, but lets us help build it.

The second mile is the best mile. It's not only relational, it is *incarnational*. That is where God shows up, often in unexpected ways. That's where the transformation happens for them — and for you.

Questions for Reflection and Discussion

Ideally, this book will be read by a group of people: a parish or diocesan staff, a group of leaders involved in parish youth ministry, Catholic camp counselors, students studying about youth ministry, and the like. I'll offer questions at the end of each chapter to help facilitate that discussion. Even if you are reading this on your own, I encourage you to write your answers in a journal.

- When you were a teenager, who helped you fall more deeply in love with God? What were their most attractive qualities?
- How did this chapter help you see "youth ministry" in a different way?
- What word best describes your attitude toward teenagers? What are some positive qualities that you notice in them?
- What excites you about doing ministry with teenagers? What scares you?

Part 1
Sharing the Gospel

2
Witnessing at the Well

One of the most detailed descriptions of Jesus having a one-on-one "ministry moment" with someone can be found in the fourth chapter of John. Jesus encountered a Samaritan woman at a well, and she was initially suspicious (and even hostile) to him. Ven. Fulton Sheen wrote in his book *Life of Christ*:

> In this long conversation between the two, there was a progression of spiritual development which finally ended in her coming to the knowledge of Christ, the Savior. … At first Christ to her was a "Jew," then a "man," then "Sir," then a "Prophet," then "the Messiah," and at last the "Savior of the world" and "Redeemer from sin." Conversion might be rapid in some, but it was not complete in this woman until she saw that Our Lord came not to save the just, but sinners.

Though our efforts in evangelization might not happen at the same pace, they should follow the same path. This is not only a beautiful story of a woman who encounters Jesus, it is also a model of how we need to bring Jesus to others. In this part of the book, I'm going to break the story down and make applications to ministry with teenagers. First, I encourage you to take out your Bible, open to John chapter 4, say a prayer asking the Holy Spirit to hear his voice, and spend a few minutes listening to what God has to say to you through this Scripture passage. Let him speak to you before I do!

Read John 4, then come back for these reflections.

Why do I get the feeling that many of you aren't getting your Bible out and doing what I asked? C'mon, people. I'm not trying to waste your time. It is very likely that God will reveal something directly to you that is way cooler than anything that I'm about to write (that's the power of Scripture). So give the Heavenly Father an opportunity to speak directly to you and prayerfully read John chapter 4.

— *Insert your prayerful reading here* —

Thanks for trusting me. The first question at the end of this chapter is about what spoke to you in that reading, so feel free to jot down some notes so that you don't forget. Okay, now on to my reflections.

Go Out of Your Way

> [Jesus] left Judea and returned to Galilee. He had to pass through Samaria. He came to a town of Samaria called Sychar, near the plot of land that Jacob had given to his son Joseph. Jacob's well was there. Jesus, tired from his journey, sat down there at the well. It was about noon. A woman of Samaria came to draw water. (John 4:3–7)

Explanation: The first verse is interesting. It says that Jesus "had to" go through Samaria, which was located between Judea and Galilee. So yes, it was the most direct route. But no Jew would ever travel that way. They would skirt around the side of Judea by the Jordan River to make their way to Galilee. Jesus had other options.

So why would John write that Jesus "had to"? It is because he wasn't only referring to geography. He was talking about ministry. Jesus wanted to meet this woman, so he "had to" go where she was. There was no way that she was going to come to him.

Jesus gets there and sends his disciples away to buy food, leaving him alone at the well. He's tired. He's thirsty. He waits. Then, at about noon (the hottest point of the day), a woman appears to draw water.

Application: Christianity is not man's search for God; it is God's search for man. God is the one who initiates contact with us. Throughout the Old Testament, God speaks through all sorts of people: kings, queens, prophets, shepherds, men, women, young, elderly, rich, poor, and so on. Only a few directly encountered God, such as Moses and Elijah. The rest saw his mighty works and heard his voice through others.

The Gospels begin with something even more shocking. "In times past, God spoke in partial and various ways to our ancestors through the prophets; in these last days, he spoke to us through a son, whom he made heir of all things and through whom he created the universe" (Heb 1:1–2). Or, as John so eloquently put it, "The Word became flesh and made his dwelling among us" (Jn 1:14).

Why? Why would the God of the Universe become human and come to us?

Because he "had to" in order to save us.

Just as we "have to" go to teenagers to bring Jesus to

them. Pope Francis wrote, "If we can hear what the Spirit is saying to us, we have to realize that youth ministry is always missionary" (*Christus Vivit*, 240). It is better to think of ourselves as "youth missionaries" than "youth ministers."

Wait at the Well

> Jacob's well was there. Jesus, tired from his journey, sat down there at the well. It was about noon. A woman of Samaria came to draw water. ... His disciples had gone into the town to buy food. (Jn 4:6–8)

Explanation: It is easy to take plumbing and running water for granted ... until it stops.

We once had a water main break in our town. They brought water trucks to our neighborhood. We all lined up, buckets in hand, to get the water that we needed to cook food, wash, or even drink. The truck was parked two blocks away, and there was always a line. It was a lot of work to carry those buckets back and forth.

IT IS BETTER TO THINK OF OURSELVES AS "YOUTH MISSIONARIES" THAN "YOUTH MINISTERS."

I tried my best not to complain during that time, knowing that there are many parts of the world that don't have running water. When I visited people in the mountain villages in Haiti, I learned that much of their day was spent carrying water back and forth. Villages were established near wells or rivers so that they could get the water they needed without having to travel too much of a distance. Water is life.

In the time of Jesus, it was the same. Towns that weren't near a natural water source needed large wells to survive. That is where Jesus, in the heat of the day, sat down to rest by himself while he sent the disciples into the town to buy food. I'm sure that they wondered why he wanted to be left behind, but they had learned not to question him. He always had a reason.

Application: For the people of Sychar, the well was their source of life. Where is the source of life for a teenager?

I think that it is reasonable to say that their "well" is their junior high or high school. It is there that many teenagers' lives are defined: smart or dumb, popular or un-popular, athletic or weak, successful or a failure, and so forth. Teenagers often spend more time at school (in both classes and activities) than adults do at their place of work, and the events continue into the weekend. Most teens would identify as being from "Indian Creek High School" more than "Blessed Sacrament Parish."

Just as Jesus "had to" go to the well in Samaria, we have to find ways to be present at the schools of the teens we accompany. We need to show up at the things that are important to them: a sporting event, a concert, a play, and so forth. This is a powerful witness of love.

There can be other "wells," too. I always had a great ministry with teens who played Dungeons and Dragons (because yes, I am *that* cool). It might sound silly to an adult, but for some teenagers, playing RPGs (role playing games) was their *identity*. Social media accounts can also be a "well" for some. Following them and liking what they post (the appropriate stuff, obviously) can make a friend for life. (This assumes that you follow the safe environment policies of your diocese — more on that in the second part of this book.)

As disciples, we know that our true identity is as a son or daughter of God. The Church, the dispenser of the mysteries of God, is our "well." If we want them to hear about *our* well, we have to start at theirs.

Then we wait. Jesus didn't go to a well where a woman was

already drawing water. He waited at the well — we don't know how long — until she showed up. Fun fact: This is the *only* Scripture that describes Jesus as "tired." Reaching the lost by going where they are is neither comfortable nor easy. Pope Francis wisely wrote, "Evangelization consists mostly of patience and disregard for constraints of time" (*Evangelii Gaudium,* 24). I've always been fascinated that of all the adjectives Saint Paul used to describe the love of God, the first on his list was "Love is patient" (1 Cor 13:4). We need to be patient and wait, not expecting immediate results, but confident that we will eventually encounter someone who is looking for something more.

REACHING THE LOST BY GOING WHERE THEY ARE IS NEITHER COMFORTABLE NOR EASY.

Cross Cultural Barriers

> A woman of Samaria came to draw water. Jesus said to her, "Give me a drink." … The Samaritan woman said to him, "How can you, a Jew, ask me, a Samaritan woman, for a drink?" (For Jews use nothing in common with Samaritans.) Jesus answered and said to her, "If you knew the gift of God and who is saying to you, 'Give me a drink,' you would have asked him and he would have given you living water." [The woman] said to him, "Sir, you do not even have a bucket and the well is deep; where then can you get this living water? Are you greater than our father Jacob, who gave us this well and drank from it himself with his children and his flocks?" (John 4:7, 9–12)

Explanation: It would have been odd enough in that time for a man to address a woman without her husband around. But for a *Jewish* man to talk to a *Samaritan* woman? Shocking!

The Jews often referred to Samaritans as "half-breeds" or "dogs," and the Samaritans felt the same way about the Jews. The Samaritans were originally Israelites until the time of the exile, when many of them intermarried with one of the great enemies of the Jewish people, the Assyrians. Samaritans believed in the Torah but not in the other sacred books. Their religious practices were intermingled with pagan ones. As was said of them in 2 Kings: "They were both venerating the LORD and serving their own gods. They followed the custom of the nations from among whom they had been deported" (17:33). For a Jew, it was better to be a pagan than a Samaritan. A Jew wouldn't even use a utensil that had been used by a Samaritan (this is why the woman comments, "You do not even have a bucket"). One might wonder what experience the Jewish disciples had, trying to purchase food in a Samaritan town!

With all those differences, what might Jesus and this woman have in common? They were both thirsty. Jesus initiated the conversation by asking for a drink. With incredible humility, Jesus put himself in a situation where he needed *her* help. She recoiled with shock, but Jesus was unfazed by this. He slowly moved the conversation from something natural to something spiritual.

Application: There is a cultural chasm between adults and teenagers. Adults don't spend time with teenagers they aren't related to unless there is a specific job involved: teacher, coach, and the like. It is true that great relationships can flourish there, but they are often performance-based. If you don't do well in the sport, you get cut from the team. If you don't do well in the class, you might be sent to a different teacher.

Teenagers can be understandably suspicious when adults like us show up at their events. If their parents and family members find it difficult to show up to the events that a teenager does at school, why would a "stranger" be there? It took me a while to convince some students that I was neither selling drugs nor an undercover cop.

Though we have many differences, we need to initiate conversations based on things that we have in common. My love of sci-fi and comic books was a great foot in the door. For others, it was sports, books, hobbies, and so forth. Just having a "normal" conversation is a win.

Humility is important. We need to be willing to learn about what they love, just as we share with them what we love. In these conversations, we approach them as peers. Teens are used to adults pulling out the "authority card." When we don't, it makes them start to wonder if we just might be for real. For example, we had decided in our ministry that high school students would call us by our first names. Though that might not work in every culture or situation, it made a big impression on the teens we ministered with. Most of them had never been on a first-name basis with an adult outside their family before.

It is good to expand your knowledge of what young people are into for the sake of ministry. However, never pretend to enjoy something you don't. I had a group of teens who were huge New York Giants fans. Having moved to Tampa in my late teenage years, I rooted for the Buccaneers. So … I found something else in common! Though we trash-talked during the season, at least we shared a love of football, and they could tell that I was genuine.

You may be in a situation ministering to teens who have a different ethnic culture than you. I am white, and in the beginning of my ministry, I had little experience with other ethnicities. I hope you know that not all Hispanics are Mexican, not all Blacks are African-American, and not all Asians are Filipino (and many Filipinos do not consider themselves Asians but Pacific Islanders or Filipino-Americans).

Avoid stereotypes, don't make assumptions, and listen eagerly when teens share about their culture. Young people are far more used to multicultural environments than older generations. I would also suggest in your initial conversations that you not give too much attention to cultural differences unless they bring it up. (Avoid saying things like, "What does your name mean?" or "How does your hair do that?") Teenagers, especially younger adolescents, want to be seen and treated like everyone else. As your relationship with the teen grows, they will likely share about their ethnicity. That is the natural time to ask questions and be open to learning. It is also an important time to affirm the beauty of their ethnic background, as sadly there are a number of teens who may be embarrassed by it or even want to reject it because they'd rather be "American."

Whether it be silly (rival sports teams) or significant (different ethnic backgrounds), adults have to willingly — and even joyfully — cross many cultural barriers to meet teenagers "where they are at" to begin the ministry of presence and accompaniment.

Questions for Reflection and Discussion

- When you read John 4 on your own, what stood out to you? If the story was familiar to you, was there something about the story that you didn't realize before?
- How does your understanding of "youth ministry" change when you replace "youth minister" with "youth missionary"?
- What do you think are the "wells" of the teens that you minister with?
- This chapter highlighted three things that Jesus did with the woman at the well: He went out of his way, he waited, and he crossed numerous cultural barriers to start a conversation with her. Which of those three things is your biggest challenge in your minis-

try with teenagers?

- Based on your answer above, what is something practical that you can do in that area to model your ministry more effectively after Jesus in those areas?

3
From Natural to Spiritual

Jesus came to us in a natural way (human) so that he could reveal supernatural realities. He only told the crowds about being the bread of life *after* he gave them bread and fish to eat (see John 6). In the first half of John 4, he didn't flash his "God" card for the Samaritan woman — he did nothing miraculous. It was well within his power (and his right) to float in the air, transfigure himself in glory, and tell the woman to bow down and worship him. Instead, he sat by a well on a hot day in a foreign land and waited for her to appear. It's nothing that we couldn't do ourselves.

Only after Jesus asks her for something and begins a conversation with her does she ask him for something: "Sir, give me this water" (Jn 4:15). She moves from sarcasm to sincerity. Now the deeper conversation can begin.

Speak First to the *Felt* Need

> Jesus answered and said to her, "Everyone who drinks this water will be thirsty again; but whoever drinks the

> water I shall give will never thirst; the water I shall give will become in him a spring of water welling up to eternal life." The woman said to him, "Sir, give me this water, so that I may not be thirsty or have to keep coming here to draw water." (John 4:13–15)

Explanation: Earlier in this Scripture story we learned that it was "about noon" when the woman came to the well. In that culture, this would have been strange. Women usually gathered water at the well in the first hours of the day so that they could have what they needed for the rest of the day. Also, depending on the time of year, it could get very hot by midday, so it made sense to do the physical labor of carrying water when it was a bit cooler outside. Why would this woman come so late in the day? She may have had some kind of water emergency. Perhaps her bucket broke or something spilled. If that were the case, then why not bring a friend or older child to help?

It is more likely that she was ostracized by her community and was trying to avoid them. The well was a place for community. Women would bring their children to the well at the start of the day, where they would talk about life while their kids played with each other. Before there were water coolers or social media, there were wells. As we are about to hear later in the story, there were scandalous things in the Samaritan woman's life that were likely a constant source of "conversation" among the other women of the town. So, she avoided them and waited until she thought she could get her water alone.

You can imagine her shock when she saw a Jewish man sitting there. She likely wanted to turn and flee, but she *needed* that stupid water, and it was only going to get hotter as the day went on. So the conversation began. She wasn't interested in this man who was thirsty and thought that he was the "gift of God," but her attitude changed when he seemed to offer her the thing that she wanted the most: to never have to come to this well again.

Application: People often think that ministry is about people coming to you to find the answers. Jesus modeled the opposite: We go to them to find their questions.

About ten years ago, we had a staffing shortage at our health center on campus at Franciscan University of Steubenville. Doctors and nurse practitioners met with sick students as quickly as they could, usually prescribing amoxicillin, the "Swiss-army knife" of antibiotics. Students began to joke that if you showed up at the health center covered in blood and suffering from multiple gunshot wounds, they'd pretend to listen and prescribe amoxicillin.

PEOPLE OFTEN THINK THAT MINISTRY IS ABOUT PEOPLE COMING TO YOU TO FIND THE ANSWERS. JESUS MODELED THE OPPOSITE: WE GO TO THEM TO FIND THEIR QUESTIONS.

Sadly, many young people have had that experience within the Church. The answer to everything is "Jesus," right? They think that asking the Church a question is about as useful as talking to a Magic 8 Ball. Except instead of the answers being "Yes," "No," and "Maybe so," they are, "You should pray more," "Go to confession," and "Because the Church says so." I admit that in my own ministry there have been times when I stopped listening and contributed to that stereotype.

Just as amoxicillin was probably the right medication for those students, Jesus *is* the answer that young people are looking for. As his disciples, we know that there is nothing more important than having a relationship with Jesus, for God gives everything else meaning and purpose. They need that relationship to experience "life and have it more abundantly" (Jn 10:10).

But that might not be their *felt* need.

Another medical analogy: You break your leg and go to the ER. During the bone scan, they detect something far more serious: leukemia. The doctor comes in, shares the bad news, and explains treatment options of radiation and chemotherapy. However, if you are screaming in pain because your bone is sticking out of your skin and nobody has done anything to fix it, you aren't able to hear what the doctor is saying above the noise of your own pain. Fix the immediate need first. Then move on to something potentially more serious.

Teens won't pay attention to the four reasons for the Incarnation if they feel depressed and isolated. They won't be interested in the commandments to love God and neighbor if their parents are going through a divorce. They won't care about the form and matter of the Sacrament of Confirmation if their boyfriend or girlfriend just broke their heart. And they certainly won't pay attention to the Church's teaching on sexuality if they have any type of same-sex attraction and assume that the Church's answer is, "Get used to being lonely."

Failing to hear the felt need of teenagers is one of the biggest reasons why so much of our ministry with youths does not bear fruit. We can get so obsessed with our spiritual answers that we become oblivious to their natural questions. No, they won't write those down and put them in a suggestion box. The real questions of the heart can only be heard in the context of genuine relationships.

Grace Builds on Nature

Abraham Maslow was an American psychologist who explained human motivation based on different levels of needs. Stacked like a pyramid, each need is dependent on the other.

Maslow proposed that the first need is *physiological:* food, water, clothing, shelter, and the like. Don't take this need for granted. Even in areas that might appear to be more affluent than others there are always teens and families that are struggling with finances. Some fear that they can't afford all the fun trips they see the youth group go on ... so why bother getting involved? Something as simple as offering lots of good food at a youth event can be an incredible gift to a teenager.

The next need in Maslow's hierarchy is *safety, protection, and security*. Do teens feel safe at home, at school, at work, or at the places they hang out? "Feel safe" is a wide phrase that covers anything from physical abuse to emotional abuse, pressures (from peers or adults) to do what they don't want, or environments that trigger anxiety. These fears for safety will motivate them to action (or inaction), whether they are based on real or imagined threats.

Maslow was an atheist and didn't put any spiritual needs in his hierarchy, so let's add some elements that he didn't. Do teens feel safe and secure in the Church? Do they feel safe with God, or are they afraid that he will send them to hell? Are they worried about being abused by a priest? Are they thinking that they will be judged by the community? Again, the brain doesn't distinguish between real or imagined dangers. Fear is fear, and it is a powerful motivator.

Many ministries focus on fulfilling the next three needs that Maslow proposes: *belongingness and love* (being a part of a family and community), *esteem* (respect from others for ourselves), and *self-actualization* (a Catholic rephrase could be "living the fullness of your vocation"). Those needs are important! But there are a lot of teens, and I stress *a lot*, who struggle with the first two. The other things won't matter unless those first needs are met.

This is why we have to go to them. Wait where they are. Cross cultural barriers. Find their felt need. It is difficult, it is uncomfortable, but there is no shortcut. It is the way that Jesus showed us. It is the way that *works*.

The Problem of Sin

> Jesus said to her, "Go call your husband and come back." The woman answered and said to him, "I do not have a husband." Jesus answered her, "You are right in saying, 'I do not have a husband.' For you have had five husbands, and the one you have now is not your husband. What you have said is true." The woman said to him, "Sir, I can see that you are a prophet." (John 4:16–19)

Explanation: The Book of Deuteronomy (part of the Torah that Samaritans also believed) stated, "When a man, after marrying a woman, is later displeased with her because he finds in her something indecent, and he writes out a bill of divorce and hands it to her, thus dismissing her from his house" (24:1). The phrase "finds in her something indecent" is vague, and it is debated whether the man needed a legitimate cause (such as the wife sleeping with another man) or if he could dismiss her because he simply didn't like her behavior. Either way, the power of divorce was in the hands of the man. Women could neither create nor break contracts.

In that time and culture, a woman divorced was a woman rejected. In the case of the Samaritan woman, perhaps some of her husbands had died. We do not know, though it is unlikely that all or even most of them did. She had suffered loss and rejection from five men and now lived with a sixth. Either the man with whom she was currently living was unwilling to take her as his wife, or she left her previous husband unlawfully. Her life was marred by tragedy, sin, and sorrow.

It is no wonder that, when asked about her husband, she replied, "I do not have a husband." This was true, but not the full truth. This made her realize that "you are a prophet" (Jn 4:19). Fulton Sheen commented in *Life of Christ*, "No physical miracle was performed; no healing, not opening of blind eyes. The wonder wrought was in a sinful soul."

There is a deeper meaning to what Jesus told her. In the Old Testament, God compared his people to a prostitute who had left him for other men. "Accuse your mother, accuse! / for she is not my wife, / and I am not her husband" (Hos 2:4). So when Jesus said, "The one you have now is not your husband," this could also be seen as a reference to himself.

Application: Jesus didn't start the conversation at the well with, "You are such a sinner!" It is only midway through the conversation that Jesus brings up sin at all. Wouldn't this have been a good moment to explain the importance of the marriage covenant and the consequences for breaking it? Shouldn't he articulate how she is living a life of sin by breaking the sixth commandment?

God detests sin. It is contrary to his very being, which is love. But he doesn't hate sin because it arbitrarily ticks him off. He hates sin because sin destroys our lives, and God loves us. Sin is the source of our misery. Jesus went to the cross so that we would no longer live under the shadow of sin. "For the wages of sin is death, but the gift of God is eternal life in Christ Jesus our Lord" (Rom 6:23). However, he wants to do more than to "fix" us and send us on our way. He desires an intimate and loving relationship with us — the imagery that Scripture uses is *marriage*. Can that relationship begin even while we are mired in our sin? Of course it can. In fact, that is the very thing that sets us free. To say otherwise would be as foolish as suggesting that we should only take the medicine after we are cured of the disease.

There are two extremes that need to be avoided. The first is to identify a teenager by his or her sin. One title for the Devil is "the accuser of our brothers" (Rv 12:10), and he would incite us to point our fingers at teenagers and say, "That one does drugs!" "That one looks at porn!" "That one is a hypocrite!" "That one is gay!" He would like us to think that some sins are just plain unforgivable, as if there was an asterisk to God's grace. The other extreme is to reduce the seriousness of sin to innocuous activity, some "poor choices" that maybe weren't the best idea at the time. When we minimize sin, we minimize salvation. If sin isn't that bad, who needs a Savior?

HOW CAN WE CORRECT WITHOUT JUDGING? THERE IS ONLY ONE WAY: IN THE CONTEXT OF FRIENDSHIP.

Pope Francis articulates the right approach: "One who accompanies others has to realize that each person's situation before God and their life in grace are mysteries which no one can fully know from without. The Gospel tells us to correct others and to help them to grow on the basis of a recognition of the objective evil of their actions, but without making judgments about their responsibility and culpability" (*Evangelii Gaudium*, 172). How can we correct without judging? There is only one way: in the context of friendship. I can be grateful for a friend correcting me because I know that he cares for me and wants the best for me, even though it is hard to hear. Do you want to feel righteous? Say what you want when you want. Do you want to do ministry? Say what is necessary when the other is ready to hear.

By the way, that *always* takes longer than "when we want."

At this point in their (albeit short) relationship, the woman at the well had moved from "Go away" to "Give me this water." Jesus' response was along the lines of, "If you want this living water, let's take a look at some things in your life that are keeping you from it." In a similar way, our deeper conversations with teenagers about sin should happen when the teen expresses a desire to grow closer to God. Sin is an offense against God, but why would someone care about offending someone they don't know? It is only after we "taste and see that the LORD is good" (Ps 34:9) that we realize that the other things that we have been eating are bland, unhealthy, and deadly. Without that experience, we don't know any better.

Though Jesus did something that we might think we can't do (he had prophetic knowledge of the Samaritan woman's past), there is something that we can do in these situations that Jesus couldn't. We can admit that we are sinners, too. We can say, "I may not struggle with what you are struggling with, but I understand the struggle. Thankfully, I have experienced in my own life that there is no wound that Jesus can't heal, no addiction that he can't break, no sin that he can't forgive. He wants to do the same with you."

Questions for Reflection and Discussion

- What are some of the felt needs of the teenagers you minister with?
- Do you agree with the statement "Failing to hear the 'felt need' of teenagers is one of the biggest reasons why so much of our ministry with youths does not bear fruit?" Why or why not?
- What are some "natural" things you can do in your ministry with teens that will help them be more receptive of the "supernatural"?
- What part of "The Problem of Sin" did you find most helpful? Do you have thoughts on how you might more effectively talk about sin with teens?

4

A New Way of Thinking

I love the moment when teens realize that I actually care for them, that I'm not here to judge (nor am I repulsed by their sin), and that I just want what is best for them. I also have something that they desire — a deeper understanding of God — and I love to talk about it! Then the honest questions begin.

Never have I heard a Catholic teen ask, "Who is this Jesus guy? I've never heard of him," or, "The Catholic Church? What is that?" In our American culture, teenagers almost always have some kind of stereotype of who Jesus is, what the Church teaches, and so forth. They've seen something on social media or heard something in a class that confused them. They always wondered but didn't know whom to ask, didn't want to offend, or didn't want to sound stupid. Perhaps they thought that they knew what Catholics were like: close-minded, judgmental, into fasting and suffering, always serious, and so on. Then they meet you, a joyful missionary disciple! Now they are reconsidering their previous judgments and wonder if you might have answers to some of the things that they've always wondered about.

Answering Their Questions

> The woman said to him, "Sir, I can see that you are a prophet. Our ancestors worshiped on this mountain; but you people say that the place to worship is in Jerusalem." Jesus said to her, "Believe me, woman, the hour is coming when you will worship the Father neither on this mountain nor in Jerusalem. You people worship what you do not understand; we worship what we understand, because salvation is from the Jews. But the hour is coming, and is now here, when true worshipers will worship the Father in Spirit and truth; and indeed the Father seeks such people to worship him. God is Spirit, and those who worship him must worship in Spirit and truth." (John 4:19–24)

Explanation: Samaritans worshiped on Mount Gerizim, which is where they believed that Abraham offered Isaac. The Jews believed that happened on Mount Moriah, which is where the Temple in Jerusalem was located. Though Jews and Samaritans disagreed on the place, they agreed on the principle: *Where* you worshiped was important. Now that she knew Jesus was a prophet, the Samaritan woman asked the big question: Where is the right place to worship? Who is right, the Jews or the Samaritans?

Jesus answers her question about who is right ("Salvation is from the Jews") but goes further, addressing the reason why she asked the question. In this new "hour," it is no longer about *where* one worships, but *how*. You can be on Mount Gerizim, Mount Moriah, or even by a well. The Father seeks those who worship him in Spirit and truth.

Application: Teens can ask some crazy questions! Don't be shocked by them. Instead, let them know that you are grateful that they are sharing their thoughts with you. Those who train to be counselors are taught to be a "nonjudgmental validating presence." Though we are not professional counselors (frequently remind yourself of that), this is a great attitude to have. We need to validate their openness, honesty, and dignity, and we need to listen to their concerns in a nonjudgmental way. Don't confuse "validate" with always agreeing with their ideas. You are validating the *person* and the value of the question. The opposite would be one who reacts with shock and/or shuts down the question because of how silly or stupid it is. Unfortunately, it is likely that they have had adults in their life react this way. That kind of reaction doesn't change their opinions, it just makes them decide to keep their opinions to themselves.

When answering questions about Church doctrine, be certain of your answers. They aren't simply asking what *you* think. As someone involved in Catholic youth ministry, you represent the Church. They have a right to hear what the Church reveals about their questions. Most importantly, *never* be afraid to say, "Wow, that's a great question. I don't know, but I will get back to you." That validates the depth of their question and gives you an excuse to have another conversation.

AS SOMEONE INVOLVED IN CATHOLIC YOUTH MINISTRY, YOU REPRESENT THE CHURCH. THEY HAVE A RIGHT TO HEAR WHAT THE CHURCH REVEALS ABOUT THEIR QUESTIONS.

Questions of the Heart

Your answers shouldn't just be intellectual. There are often questions behind the question, preconceived notions that they have that drive the questions they ask.

Not to flex too much, but I have a Ph.D. in theology and twenty years teaching the *Catechism* and Scripture to college students on the undergraduate and master's level. To sum up: I know stuff. However, in ministry situations, when I am asked a question about God, I take a breath and whisper, "Come, Holy Spirit." Perhaps this is a question with a simple answer, something that they are curious about. But there may be something deeper they really want to know. We should witness as we worship, not just in truth, but in *Spirit* and truth.

A few years ago, a student in one of my classes raised her hand and asked, "What do we say to someone who wonders why, if God is good, he allows suffering to exist?" This is a common question, and I've got a great theological answer. It has to do with the communal effect of sin and the role that free will plays in our relationship with God and our own salvation. We can't choose God if we can't choose against him, and our choices against him affect the people around us.

Doesn't that sound smart? I'm glad you are impressed.

As I was about to say that, the Spirit stopped me. *Don't lecture.* So I took a breath and said a quick prayer. "I don't know," I said. The students in the class looked at each other with some confusion. This was not the answer that they (or I) expected to hear.

I shared about a tragic experience in my own life. Our first pregnancy ended in a late-term miscarriage. My theology was thrown out the window. My wife and I wondered why, after dedicating our lives to God, he would let something like that happen to us. It seemed cruel. It felt unfair. Instead of walking away from God, we clung to the cross and encountered Jesus who suffered with us, drawing closer to him — and each other — than we ever had before. I still don't know why my son died before I got to hold him; I still wish it hadn't happened. But Jesus took on my suffering, my wife's suffering, and the suffering of the world.

That's what I hold on to.

At this point, I was crying a little, and this young woman was crying a lot. I gave the class a ten-minute break and sat with her. She shared that her little brother had died of cancer a few years ago. She had asked that question a few times in other classes, and in each one got a similar theological or philosophical explanation. But this was the answer that she was looking for, the one that God wanted her to hear.

That student didn't really want to know about why suffering existed. The question she really wanted to know was, "How are you supposed to trust God after you feel like he has let you down?" She didn't need to read the answer in a textbook, she needed to read it in the letter of the heart of a disciple. I was so glad that Jesus sent me to her that day.

It was likely that the people of Sychar considered the woman at the well "unclean" and therefore barred her from worshiping on the mountain, just as a Jew would bar someone unclean from the Temple in Jerusalem. If worship was about a "place," then she was unable to have a relationship with God. "Where can I pray?" was the surface question; "Does God care about me or my prayers?" was the deeper one. Jesus told her that people would worship "neither on this mountain nor in Jerusalem" (Jn 4:21) not to satisfy her theological curiosity but her spiritual longing: You *can* have a relationship with God, right where you are.

Some questions are from the mind; some questions are from the heart. Ask the Spirit to help you discern which are which. Be as honest with your witness and as accurate with Church teaching as you can. And have confidence. There is a reason that Jesus sent you to this teenager as his letter.

A disclaimer: My comments in this section refer specifically to those teens with whom we have built a friendship of trust and respect. There is a difference between someone seeking an answer and someone starting an argument. I'm not suggesting that you open your heart to someone who is holding a knife. Of those Jesus said, "Do not give what is holy to dogs, or throw your pearls before swine, lest they trample them underfoot, and turn and tear you to pieces" (Mt 7:6). Your heart is holy. Your pearls are the beauty of what God has revealed through his Church. Truth is like a scalpel: In the right hands and the right place, it can save lives. But don't bring a scalpel to a knife fight.

Be Prepared for Tough Topics

At some point, a teen might ask, "If I told you something, can you keep it secret?" The best response is something like this: "If you shared something with me that is about harming yourself or something that would harm others, then no. I care for you too much to keep that to myself." Don't press; just be present and listen. Start quietly praying, "Come, Holy Spirit," and be a nonjudgmental, validating presence as the teen shares. In my experience, they always do.

Whenever a teenager opens up his or her heart to you, it is truly sacred ground. It can also be *scary* ground. Your diocese/parish/apostolate/ministry should provide training on what to do if young people share that they are abusing themselves, being abused by others, or are in a potentially dangerous situation. When they come to us for this kind of help, we need to get them to the people who can help them, which isn't us (unless you are a licensed counselor, and even then there are others who should be involved). Make it clear that this isn't just a "handoff" to another person. You aren't abandoning them! You are acknowledging that you don't have the ability to give them the help they need, but you know those who can.

How will you respond to difficult statements? Here are a few you might hear: "I think I am gay." "I'm having sex with my boyfriend/girlfriend." "I had an abortion." "I feel like I'm a different gender." Talk this over with your ministry team. The teen who is sharing these things is likely expecting judgment and condemnation. Be the face of mercy. He or she is expecting a lecture on morality. Instead, ask about what happened, or how long he or she has felt that way. The teen probably knows what the Church teaches, but he or she likely doesn't know how the Church *responds*. Respond with love, sympathy, and compassion.

When teens share these things with you, first, thank them for being vulnerable and sharing with you. Let them know that you are praying for them, and even pray with them in that moment if it is appropriate. Perhaps they would like to have a conversation about the Church's teaching about these subjects; perhaps they just wanted to see how a Catholic might respond to someone who struggles with them. Don't go into lecture mode, but don't leave them without any next step, either. Remember, the point of accompaniment is to lead them to Jesus. So, I'd at least say something like, "I am so honored that you shared this with me. Jesus invites all of us to a new way of life, and that includes what we do with our bodies. I hope that you might be open to further conversations about that." The longer you've been accompanying that teenager, the more substantial that conversation can be.

TEENS PROBABLY KNOW WHAT THE CHURCH TEACHES, BUT THEY LIKELY DON'T KNOW HOW THE CHURCH RESPONDS. RESPOND WITH LOVE, SYMPATHY, AND COMPASSION.

It is essential that you talk with the others in your ministry about how to answer questions like these and when it would be appropriate to involve their families. Abuse situations are obvious (yes, tell them!), but sexual issues may not be as clear. Do you tell their parents/guardians if their teen is sexually active, or if they say that they are gay (assuming that their families do not know this)? Because ministries with adolescents cover such a wide range of ages (eleven to eighteen), contexts (parish youth groups to juvenile detention centers), and cultures (cultural communities have different expectations of familial involvement), one rule would not fit all.

As you discern, keep these three points in mind. First, the concern should not be for how they react but how to respond in their best interests. Second, whatever decisions are made should be clearly communicated with those involved in that ministry so that no single person bears the brunt of the decision. Finally, a young person should know ahead of time how you might react, so that they don't feel tricked. This is important to keep the relationship alive. So, if they ask, "If I tell you something, will you tell my family?" you might say, "I know your family, they are great people who care for you. So, I might, if I thought it was something that they needed to know and would be best for you. What's going on?" That way, if you do need to tell their family, you aren't breaking trust.

A New Way of Holiness

It is well beyond the scope of this book to help you address the variety of questions you might get asked. The *Catechism of the Catholic Church* is the best place to find answers to pretty much anything on the topics of doctrine and morality. Historical stuff (Crusades, Inquisition, did the Church help the Jews in World War II, etc.) is a little trickier and might require a bit of research on your part. I've heard a lot of questions that begin, "I heard it says in the Bible that ..." Nine times out of ten, the Bible said no such thing, so don't always accept the premise of the question. Again, "I don't know but I'll find out" is a great response, and it is OK if you don't know the answer the next day.

One of the most prevalent misunderstandings that teens have is about *holiness*. Many of their questions — "Is it a sin if ..." "How far is too far?" "Why do we have to ..." — stem from confusing *holiness* with *not sinning*. Let me explain the difference.

You can't define a thing by what it isn't, which is why you can't say that "not sinning" is the definition of *holiness*. Not sinning is just that: not sinning. It is a part of being holy, but not the whole. Many people think that the main point of religion is to make you a better person, or at least less of a mean one. Since Jesus is the Divine Physician, they assume that they are the Perpetual Patient. They make their appointments, get their treatment, and come back again when they get hurt. The ultimate goal is to be a good person. Or at least to not go to hell.

WE DON'T WANT TO HELP TEENS SIMPLY BE BETTER PEOPLE. WE WANT THEM TO BECOME FELLOW DISCIPLES OF JESUS CHRIST.

In this mindset, holiness ("not sinning") is not only unattainable; it is also boring. They might appreciate the lives of saints, but they certainly don't want to be one. So, when they ask, "How far is too far?" (a common question about sexual activity), they really mean, "How much fun can I have without going to hell?"

It is the wrong question. Would I ask my wife, "How much can I sin against you before you would throw me out of the house?" The very question means that I don't understand what marriage is about. It treats her like a "fun-killer" as opposed to my best friend and the love of my life. Many people have this misconception of God: the fun-killer instead of the life-giver.

We don't want to help teens simply be better people. We want them to become fellow disciples of Jesus Christ. Young people need to see the beauty of holiness. Holiness is not defined by the absence of sin but the presence of God in our lives. It is not merely a list of "thou shalt nots." It is a yes to God's invitation to be his own. Holiness is embracing the fullness of life. Look at the fruits of the Spirit: "love, joy, peace, patience, kindness, generosity, faithfulness, gentleness, self-control" (Gal 5:22–23). Who wouldn't want those? There are only ten ways to sin, but a thousand ways to be holy.

So, what of sin? Sin diminishes God's presence in our lives but doesn't remove it (unless we are unrepentant). In fact, Saint John wrote, "If we say, 'We are without sin,' we deceive ourselves, and the truth is not in us" (1 Jn 1:8). Of all the places that Saint Paul visited, Corinth was arguably the worst, and his two letters to them have some of the strongest condemnations about moral behavior. Yet he tells them, "Do you not know that you are the temple of God, and that the Spirit of God dwells in you? … For the temple of God, which you are, is holy" (1 Cor 3:16–17).

By God's grace, I am holy. I am his temple, his disciple, and his son. I still sin, and that stinks. When I do, I repent as quickly as I can and come back to his open arms. I love the phrase, "A saint is just a sinner who fell down and got up." Jesus keeps pulling us up, not just to live without sin, but to live in his love. *That* is the beauty of holiness.

As I was sharing this at a youth ministry workshop, an agitated person raised his hand. "If Jesus didn't start with sin, then why were his first words in Mark '*Repent*, and believe in the gospel?' What are they repenting from, if not from sin?" All eyes turned toward me in expectation.

I replied, "Wow, that's a great question. I don't know, but I will get back to you."

See? That is always OK to say.

I did my research. He was correct that the first words of Jesus in the Gospel of Mark are, "This is the time of fulfillment. The kingdom of God is at hand. Repent, and believe in the gospel"

(Mk 1:15). The misunderstanding was the meaning of the word *repent.* In English, this means to acknowledge that we have done something wrong and do something to make up for it. With that definition, Jesus' words could be read as, "Admit you're a sinner and stop it!"

Thankfully, Mark wasn't written in English, but in Greek. In Greek, Jesus used the word μετανοεῖτε (*metanoeite*), which literally means to "come to a new mind." Change your perspective. Reconsider the way you used to think. So, "Repent and believe the gospel" is more accurately translated as, "Think about things in a new way and believe the Good News." It doesn't start with condemnation, but invitation.

The proclamation of Jesus at the beginning of Mark's Gospel is exactly what he communicated to the woman at the well, and it is the same message that he wants us to communicate to teens: The time is now. God is here. See things in a new way. Believe.

Questions for Reflection and Discussion

- What was the most helpful thing that you got from this chapter?
- How would you explain the difference between answering the question and answering the person?
- Do you feel like there is clarity (and unity) within your ministry on how to respond to some of the "tough questions" that teenagers ask? If not, what do you think would help you get that clarity?
- What negative misconceptions do you think that the teens you minister with have about holiness, and how might you help them see it in a new, more attractive way?

Interlude: A Dream

Back in my time at the parish, I was lying in bed after a long day, praying about an upcoming retreat. I was worried about the transportation costs, the lack of registration, and what color the T-shirts should be. I must have fallen asleep in prayer, or perhaps it was a vision, because I opened my eyes and saw Jesus sitting in front of me.

He looked at me with love, a smile on his face. He asked me the same question he asked blind Bartimaeus in the Gospels: "Bob, what do you want me to do for you?"

My heart skipped a beat. "Wow, Jesus! How did you know I needed you?"

"I know the desires of your heart, Bob," he said. "You can share them with me."

I felt such relief! "Well, Jesus, then you know what I really desire is …"

Jesus leaned forward in anticipation.

"… to figure out if I should go with a red T-shirt or a charcoal gray T-shirt for the retreat."

Jesus leaned back. "What?"

"Well," I explained, "I think the red really pops, you know? But red doesn't look that good on me. I'm an English Summer … but you already knew that, didn't you?" I laughed. He didn't. I continued: "Anywho, I'm thinking the gray. That's not selfish, is it? I mean, pretty much all I wear are youth group T-shirts, so shouldn't I pick something that is more flattering on me?"

Jesus looked at me, bewildered. He didn't speak for a moment or two. I was glad that he was giving this matter the serious consideration that it deserved.

"The color of the T-shirt doesn't matter," he finally said. "What I really want —"

"So the gray would be fine then, right?" I interrupted. He shrugged, which I took as a yes and did an interior fist pump. I really liked the gray color. It was more of a dark charcoal, really. Very cool.

"Bob, don't worry about the T-shirts. Don't worry about the transportation stuff. Don't even worry about the retreat." OK, that was crazy talk, but since he is the Lord of the Universe, I let him continue. "I am here for you, Bob. For you. Now, what do you want me to do for *you*?"

"…th ministry," I finished his sentence.

"What?"

"*You*th ministry," I said.

He seemed irritated. "No, not youth ministry. You."

"…th ministry," I said again.

He forced a smile. "No, just you." He quickly held up his hand to stop me from saying anything else. I saw the hole in it. I could actually see *through* it. It occurred to me that it would make a great logo for our youth group! Then I noticed him looking at me with a deep, penetrating stare. This was getting uncomfortable.

"For *you*, Bob. Not for youth ministry. What can I do, just for *you*?"

I thought for a moment, perplexed. When he saw that I wasn't sure what to ask for, he added, "Think big."

Think big?

I considered this. What is the biggest thing that I could ask for?

"A raise?" I offered.

Jesus put his head in his hands.

Then the alarm went off and I sat up in bed. Was that real? What was Jesus trying to say to me? As the details of the dream began to fade, I clung to the one thing, the one piece of truth that I felt that Jesus was trying to say to me.

Gray T-shirts. Nailed it.

5
Sharing the Gospel

Paul, Silvanus, and Timothy lived with the faithful in the Greek city of Thessalonica, selling tents (that was their day job) and sharing Jesus. After Paul left, he wrote to the Thessalonians, saying, "With such affection for you, we were determined to share with you not only the gospel of God, but our very selves as well, so dearly beloved had you become to us" (1 Thes 2:8). How beautiful! They were *determined* to share both the Gospel and their lives with them.

We need to have the same determination in ministry. There is a difference between *saying* the Gospel and *sharing* the Gospel. Teenagers who have been to church most of their lives, or who have been through parish faith formation and sacramental formation, likely have had the Gospel "said" to them. But I propose that few have had the Gospel "shared" with them.

"Share" is also different than "give." If I am volunteering at a soup kitchen, I might *give* homeless people some food. Only when I sit down at the table can I *share* a meal with them.

In the Catholic Church's ministry with teenagers, we can too often "say" or "give" the Gospel to teenagers. We can keep them at arm's length and throw them food, like dangerous animals at a zoo. Yet the model that Jesus gives us is to "dwell among," to accompany, to break bread with, to share. The only way that we can share the Gospel is by sharing our lives.

Jesus humbled himself to wait by a well on a hot day in a hostile environment for an ostracized woman who didn't even want to talk to him in the first place. Instead of issuing commands, he gave her the dignity of having a conversation. He wanted to show the woman *who* he was before confirming *what* he was: the Messiah.

The Necessity of Words

> The woman said to him, "I know that the Messiah is coming, the one called the Anointed; when he comes, he will tell us everything." Jesus said to her, "I am he, the one who is speaking with you." (John 4:25–26)

Explanation: Like the Jews, Samaritans were waiting for the fulfillment of the prophecy spoken by Moses, "A prophet like me will the LORD, your God, raise up for you from among your own kindred; that is the one to whom you shall listen" (Dt 18:15). She was expecting the Messiah, but she wasn't expecting him to be *Jewish*. It is understandable that she didn't have the courage that Saint Peter had when he exclaimed, "You are the Messiah, the Son of the living God" (Mt 16:16). But something in her heart screamed, "It must be him!" So she made a passive statement about the Messiah, hoping that he might say something about it.

He did. "I am he."

Application: Jesus had a very unorthodox marketing strategy.

His goal was to reveal himself to the world. If I were his

agent, I'd propose a worldwide tour with lots of flashy miracles. Jesus wasn't interested in any of that. Most of his ministry happened within twelve square miles in Galilee, and the rest took place in a geographical area smaller than the state of Connecticut. He often healed people in private (like the raising of Jairus's daughter) and didn't even let all the Apostles see what was arguably his "flashiest" miracle, the Transfiguration.

Jesus wanted to encounter people first and slowly reveal himself. He preferred to help people realize that he was the Christ rather than simply telling them. The Devil seemed to understand this strategy. Those who were possessed often cried out, "I know who you are — the Holy One of God!" (Mk 1:24) before Jesus silenced them. The Devil was trying to interrupt the process!

The crowd's reaction to the miraculous feeding of the five thousand men (not including women and children) gives us some insight into why Jesus did this: "Since Jesus knew that they were going to come and carry him off to make him king, he withdrew again to the mountain alone" (Jn 6:15). Obviously, that wasn't the kind of kingship that he came for.

Jesus needed to disabuse them of their conceptions of him — who they thought that he should be — before he could reveal to them who he really was. The best way to do that was in smaller settings that were more conversational than preaching, more relational than hierarchical. That is why this conversation at the well provides a perfect paradigm for evangelization. Jesus models the kind of relational ministry necessary to effectively proclaim him to the world, a method that is as counter cultural as the message. Announcing to large groups is a lot easier than accompanying individuals (especially on social media), but it doesn't make disciples.

The goal of Christian accompaniment is not to wander aimlessly with another, but to meet him where he is so as to lead him to Jesus. It takes time to show someone that we're not selling something for our benefit but sharing something for his. We earn the right to be heard so that we can say something worth hearing.

There is a quote often misattributed to St. Francis of Assisi that goes something like "Preach the Gospel at all times; if necessary use words." Though the emphasis on a wordless witness is good, since that is the first step of evangelization, many Catholics would like to translate this as, "Be a good person and then you don't have to talk about the Faith."

Saint Paul would strongly disagree. "How can they call on him in whom they have not believed? And how can they believe in him of whom they have not heard? And how can they hear without someone to preach? … Thus faith comes from what is heard, and what is heard comes through the word of Christ" (Rom 10:14, 17). The question is not "if" words are necessary, but "when."

THE QUESTION IS NOT "IF" WORDS ARE NECESSARY, BUT "WHEN."

The Kerygma

In Greek, the word kerygma means "message," and it is the word that the Church uses to capture the richness of the Good News that Jesus proclaimed through both word and deed. Though it always involves distinct elements, Pope Francis cautioned, "We should not think, however, that the Gospel message must always be communicated by fixed formulations learned by heart or by specific words which express an absolutely invariable content" (*Evangelii Gaudium*, 129).

Saint Peter wrote, "Sanctify Christ as Lord in your hearts. Always be ready to give an explanation to anyone who asks you for a reason for your hope" (1 Pt 3:15). Our explanation isn't something that we recite from a note card, but something that we share from the letter of our heart.

I think that Pope Francis offers the simplest expression of the kerygma, one that I often use when speaking to teens: "Jesus Christ loves you; he gave his life to save you; and now he is living at your side every day to enlighten, strengthen and free you" (*Evangelii Gaudium*, 164).

"Jesus Christ Loves You"

"For God so loved the world …" begins the most famous passage of Scripture, John 3:16. The entire motivation of God is love. Saint John takes this a step even further, saying, "God is love, and whoever remains in love remains in God and God in him" (1 Jn 4:16).

The Greek word for *love* used in the Gospels was *agapē*, which was more than just emotional affection. It was an unwavering commitment for the good of the other, even to the point of self-sacrifice. This is the way that God loves us, for "No one has greater love than this, to lay down one's life for one's friends" (Jn 15:13). Saint Paul marveled, "What then shall we say to this? If God is for us, who can be against us? He who did not spare his own Son but handed him over for us all, how will he not also give us everything else along with him?" (Rom 8:31–32).

"In this way the love of God was revealed to us: God sent his only Son into the world so that we might have life through him" (1 Jn 4:9). Understanding that we are unconditionally loved by Jesus, the image of the invisible God who reveals to us the love of the Father and the Holy Spirit, is the foundation of the kerygma. I was at a concert with one of my favorite Christian musicians, Rich Mullins, and he made this bold statement: "There is nothing you can do that can make God love you more, and there is nothing you can do that can make God love you less." It sounds scandalous, doesn't it? When I share that quote with teenagers,

I often see the eyes of adults grow wide with shock. Some even slightly shake their head, signaling to me that I've gone too far.

More accurately, it could be said that *God* went too far by becoming flesh and dwelling among us. It was a reckless act, and one that got him killed! He did it because "God so loved the world." His love can neither be earned nor lost. Even when we deny it, his love keeps coming after us. "It bears all things, believes all things, hopes all things, endures all things. Love never fails" (1 Cor 13:7–8).

Teens can experience God's love in a new way when we take the time to build relationships with them. Very few teenagers have experienced the love of an adult who wasn't a family member or who didn't want something from them. Like God, we love them for who they are, not what they've done. As they wonder why we care for them, we give them the "reason for your hope": God loves us all, no matter what.

"God is love" (1 Jn 4:16). The invitation to love him in return is open to everyone! Sadly, many reject that invitation. And that is why …

"He Gave His Life to Save You"

The sin of our first parents, Adam and Eve, contaminated the human race forever. "For there is no distinction; all have sinned and are deprived of the glory of God" (Rom 3:22–23). The *Catechism* states, "Sin is present in human history; any attempt to ignore it or to give this dark reality other names would be futile" (386). We have to clearly point this out. "Without the knowledge Revelation gives of God we cannot recognize sin clearly and are tempted to explain it as merely a developmental flaw, a psychological weakness, a mistake, or the necessary consequence of an inadequate social structure, etc." (387). This is why it is important that the Holy Spirit "convict the world in regard to sin and righteousness and condemnation" (Jn 16:8), otherwise we would shrug our shoulders, mutter, "Nobody's perfect," and move on.

Sin is serious. *Deadly* serious. It isn't like catching a cold or pulling a muscle. It is a fatal cancer. It is cutting an artery. It is not something that you can recover from on your own. Without a cure, you will die from it. Just as sin brought physical death into the world, it also brought a spiritual death: eternal separation from God. This is known as "hell."

The *Catechism* states, "The teaching of the Church affirms the existence of hell and its eternity. … The chief punishment of hell is eternal separation from God, in whom alone man can possess the life and happiness for which he was created and for which he longs" (1035). Jesus frequently mentioned that hell was a consequence for those who refused to repent and turn from their selfish, worldly desires. Sadly, that is where many end up. "Enter through the narrow gate; for the gate is wide and the road broad that leads to destruction, and those who enter through it are many. How narrow the gate and constricted the road that leads to life. And those who find it are few" (Mt 7:13–14).

Woah, hold on, you might complain. *What happened to all the "God loves you" stuff?* He does! And do you want to know the best way he shows that?

He saves us from hell.

Jesus didn't give his life for me so that I would simply be a nicer person or have a more positive mental attitude. "The temptation today is to reduce Christianity to merely human wisdom, a pseudo-science of well-being" (*Redemptoris Missio,* 11). It is so much more than that! Jesus died on the cross so that you and I could be with him forever in eternity. "For God so loved the world that he gave his only Son, so that everyone who believes in him might not perish but might have eternal life" (Jn 3:16).

Eternal life! It will be more than naked babies playing harps in clouds. "Heaven is the blessed community of all who are perfectly incorporated into Christ. This mystery of blessed communion with God and all who are in Christ is beyond all understanding and description" (CCC 1026–1027). It is a level of awesomeness that we can't even imagine!

"For the wages of sin is death, but the gift of God is eternal life in Christ Jesus our Lord" (Rom 6:23). This is the drama of salvation history. The Gospel is the "Good News." But the Good News isn't good if the bad news isn't bad. If sin isn't severe, then salvation isn't that valuable, and that diminishes what Jesus did for us on the cross. Remember what we've already discussed in reflecting on John chapter 4. There is a time and place to address sin, and that usually isn't the start of the conversation. But it has to be addressed eventually, as guided by the Spirit, because sin keeps us from the fullness of life that God wants for us.

THE GOSPEL IS THE "GOOD NEWS." BUT THE GOOD NEWS ISN'T GOOD IF THE BAD NEWS ISN'T BAD.

When the Spirit convicts us of our sin, he does so in a way that doesn't dilute our dignity. "For godly sorrow produces a salutary repentance without regret, but worldly sorrow produces death" (2 Cor 7:10). The Devil, the "accuser of our brothers" (Rv 12:10), wants us to feel shame: "I am wrong, there is nothing good about me." The Spirit brings "godly sorrow" that leads to mercy: "I did something wrong, but I am loved by God who rejoices when I turn back to him." For Jesus said, "I tell you, in just the same way there will be more joy in heaven over one sinner who repents than over ninety-nine righteous people who have no need of repentance" (Lk 15:7).

Oh, how I wish more Catholics understood this! "Catholic guilt" isn't found in the Bible, just in our own prideful hearts when we fail to accept the fullness of God's mercy. The word regret literally means to "weep again," to live in our past sins and failings. That's not where God wants us to be. We must believe and rejoice that, "as far as the east is from the west, / so far has he removed our sins from us" (Ps 103:12).

To help young people understand what it means when we say, "Jesus gave his life to save you," we have to be able to explain what we were saved from and what we are saved for. Jesus gave his life to save us from sin and death and for a life of freedom and communion with God, both now and in the life to come. He gave his life to save us!

"And Now He Is Living at Your Side"

Loving us and giving his life to save us should be more than enough, right? We would not dare to ask for anything else. Yet God continues to be overwhelmingly generous and merciful, as Pope Francis reminds us: "And now he is living at your side every day to enlighten, strengthen and free you."

It is fun to think of Jesus as a superhero, leaving his throne in heaven to swoop down, punch the Devil in the face, and save his people from their sins. Here's the problem with that analogy: Superheroes don't stick around when the job is done. They tell you to be safe and fly off to their next adventure. It would be odd if Superman saved someone falling from a building, gently brought them down to earth, and then asked, "So, what's for dinner?"

A survey from the beginning of the twenty-first century found that the majority of teenagers think that "God is something like a combination Divine Butler and Cosmic Therapist: He is always on call, takes care of any problems that arise, professionally helps his people to feel better about themselves, and does not become too personally involved in the process." I know that a lot has changed in youth culture since that survey, but I think that description is still accurate.

Many believe that God created the world and even shows up

occasionally. They are far less likely to believe what Jesus said at the conclusion of Gospel of Matthew: "And behold, I am with you always, until the end of the age" (Mt 28:20). Those words harken back to the beginning of Matthew's Gospel when he quotes from Isaiah, "'Behold, the virgin shall be with child and bear a son, and they shall name him Emmanuel,' which means 'God is with us'" (Mt 1:23). Our faith is not historical information about a time that God *was* with us, but a joyful proclamation that God *is* with us, and is with us "always." Not sometimes. Not occasionally. Not just in church or on retreat. *Always.* This is why Pope Francis begins his exhortation to young people by exclaiming, "Christ is alive!" (*Christus Vivit*, 1).

OUR FAITH IS NOT HISTORICAL INFORMATION ABOUT A TIME THAT GOD WAS WITH US, BUT A JOYFUL PROCLAMATION THAT GOD IS WITH US, AND IS WITH US "ALWAYS."

The shocking truth is that Jesus not only loves us, he also *likes* us. He wants to spend time with us. He knows everything about us, for "even the hairs of your head have all been counted" (Lk 12:7, spoken to a group of people who had long hair and full beards). "For you love all things that are / and loathe nothing that you have made" (Wis 11:24).

Though I can't see him, Jesus is with me as I'm writing this (and with you as you are reading). However, he is not always invisible. Jesus makes himself tangibly present to us in numerous ways through his Church:

> "Christ Jesus, who died, yes, who was raised from the dead, who is at the right hand of God, who indeed intercedes for us," is present in many ways to his Church:

> in his word, in his Church's prayer, "where two or three are gathered in my name," in the poor, the sick, and the imprisoned, in the sacraments of which he is the author, in the sacrifice of the Mass, and in the person of the minister. But "he is present … most *especially in the Eucharistic species*." (CCC 1373)

The Church is not just the building that you go to so that you can receive the sacraments. Nor is it simply a place where old men with pointy hats go to work. "The Church is essentially both human and divine, visible but endowed with invisible realities" (*Sacrosanctum Concilium*, 2). The Church is the People of God, the Body of Christ, the Bride of Christ, and the Temple of the Holy Spirit, "one complex reality which comes together from a human and a divine element" (*Lumen Gentium*, 8).

When you read the Gospels and the Acts of the Apostles, it is clear that the Church was not an afterthought of Jesus, or a "Jesus Fan Club" put together by those left behind after his ascension. By gathering the apostles and putting Peter at their head, Jesus established the Church so that he would continually be present through her. "Just as God's will is creation and is called 'the world,' so his intention is the salvation of men, and it is called 'the Church'" (CCC 760).

Because she is made of sinful people, like you and me, the Church's members can do great harm. This is not to be taken lightly. "The Church, embracing in its bosom sinners, at the same time holy and always in need of being purified, always follows the way of penance and renewal" (*Lumen Gentium*, 8). To reject the Church is to reject Christ, because "Christ loved the church and handed himself over for her to sanctify her, cleansing her by the bath of water with the word, that he might present to himself the church in splendor, without spot or wrinkle or any such thing, that she might be holy and without blemish" (Eph

5:25–27). It is *through* the Church that Jesus sanctifies us and is present to us. As Pope Benedict XVI said, "The Church does not exist for her own sake, she is not the point of arrival, but she has to point upwards, beyond herself, to the realms above."

Without the reality of the Church, our understanding of and relationship with Jesus is in danger of becoming fantasy — something imagined, not tangible. Without the Church, the Gospel is merely an inspirational story from the past. Within the Church, Jesus is alive and present to "enlighten, strengthen and free you." We are enlightened by her teaching, strengthened in her community, and freed from sin through her sacraments.

Jesus loves us, Jesus died for our sins, and Jesus is with us. One could argue that calling this the "Good News" is an understatement. This is the best possible news, beyond our wildest imagination! This is the kerygma that we share with teens as we share our lives. If we truly love them, why would we keep it to ourselves?

Over and Over

Personally, my favorite ministry moments are when I get to share the kerygma for the first time with a teen who has never heard it before. I have seen it dramatically change lives, just as it dramatically changed mine. But it shouldn't be only said once and never again. Pope Francis said that this proclamation "must ring out over and over" (*Evangelii Gaudium*, 164). I return to it again and again, reminding the teens with whom I work that they are always loved by God, that his mercy never comes to an end, and that he is always present with us. I think that Pope Francis said it best when he wrote:

> The centrality of the kerygma calls for stressing those elements which are most needed today: it has to express God's saving love which precedes any moral and

> religious obligation on our part; it should not impose the truth but appeal to freedom; it should be marked by joy, encouragement, liveliness and a harmonious balance which will not reduce preaching to a few doctrines which are at times more philosophical than evangelical. All this demands on the part of the evangelizer certain attitudes which foster openness to the message: approachability, readiness for dialogue, patience, a warmth and welcome which is nonjudgmental. (*Evangelii Gaudium*, 165)

Proclaiming the kerygma is a high moment, but certainly not the final one. It elevates the journey that we are on with teenagers because it becomes a fork in the road, a potential change of direction, where a teen can decide to walk toward Jesus and his Church (especially if they were heading in the opposite direction). Our lives are like highways with multiple exits. They aren't unlimited (because we live finite lives on earth), but there is always another if you miss one. Sometimes you have to pass a few exits with a teen before they decide to take the turn that God is calling them to.

Sadly, there are teens who, at least while we are available to them, won't take the path of discipleship. I try my best not to break off my relationship with those who decide not to follow in the footsteps of Jesus, but I find that they often break their relationship with me. They stop coming to events, don't respond when I reach out, and sometimes even actively avoid me at school activities. It can be heartbreaking.

This is part of the life of ministry. I often worry that I did something wrong, and it is always a good thing to reflect on what happened and learn from any mistakes I might have made. However, there were people who even turned away from Jesus during his earthly ministry, so I can't assume that I will do any better than he did. I keep those teenagers in prayer and have hope that something I said or did might have planted a seed in their heart that will later bloom.

Empowering Teens to Be Missionaries

> The woman left her water jar and went into the town. … Many of the Samaritans of that town began to believe in him because of the word of the woman who testified, "He told me everything I have done." When the Samaritans came to him, they invited him to stay with them; and he stayed there two days. Many more began to believe in him because of his word, and they said to the woman, "We no longer believe because of your word; for we have heard for ourselves, and we know that this is truly the savior of the world." (John 4:28, 39–42)

Explanation: Jesus is the Messiah! The Samaritan woman is so excited to tell others about him that she leaves her water jar behind. Jesus didn't even have to say, "Now go and tell the people in your town about me." It was the natural thing to do, even though these were the same people who had ostracized her for her sinfulness.

They were likely moved not just by the words that were spoken but the change that they saw in her. This was not the same woman who avoided crowds and snuck off at odd hours to get water. Something had happened to her, and the people of the town were curious to see what that was.

"They invited him to stay with them." This shouldn't be overlooked — Samaritans inviting a group of Jews to stay with them? Unheard of. But they did this because of her witness. It is a beautiful example of the words written by Pope St. Paul VI, "for the Church, the first means of evangelization is the witness of an authentically Christian life. … Modern man listens more willingly to witnesses than to teachers, and if he does listen to teachers, it is because they are witnesses" (*Evangelii Nuntiandi*, 41).

Application: Have you wondered what this woman's name was? History tells us that her name was Photini (or at least that was her baptized name), which means "light." She continued to preach the Gospel to others and was eventually martyred by Emperor Nero. The Church used to celebrate the feast of Saint Photini on March 20, until the liturgical calendar was updated (though she is still considered a saint).

Why didn't John use her actual name? It is unlikely that he forgot it. Another prominent unnamed character in his Gospel is "the disciple whom Jesus loved." This was obviously John himself. Why didn't he say so? It may have been his humility. However, it is more likely that John intentionally remained anonymous to put the *reader* into the story. By removing his name, he allowed *us* to see ourselves as that disciple.

In a similar way, John also invites us to see ourselves as the woman at the well. *We* become the ones who have a profound encounter with Jesus and then run off to tell others about it. Though we may initially convince others because of our witness and words, the real conversion happens when they encounter Jesus for themselves. We are there to arouse their curiosity and facilitate that introduction. Jesus takes care of the rest.

When I look back over my past thirty years of ministry, I am so grateful that Jesus used someone as unworthy as me to introduce so many teenagers to him. Like the woman, I was an outcast and a sinner, living day to day on stagnant water that never actually quenched my thirst. Then he came to me, and everything changed. Now I don't just want to tell everyone about it, I *need* to. My heart resonates with the words of Saint Paul: "If I preach the gospel, this is no reason for me to boast, for an obligation has been imposed on me, and woe to me if I do not preach it!" (1 Cor 9:16).

Teenagers need to be invited into that mission and be given many opportunities to do it. If they aren't comfortable serving those in need and sharing their faith with their peers while they are in high school, it is unlikely that they will do so on their own in college or at work. Pope St. Paul VI wrote, "Here lies the test of truth, the touchstone of evangelization: it is unthinkable that a person should accept the Word and give himself to the kingdom without becoming a person who bears witness to it and proclaims it in his turn" (*Evangelii Nuntiandi*, 24). You can argue that if someone isn't on fire to share this message with others, then he or she doesn't fully understand what it means.

Like Saint Photini, some teenagers come home from a camp or retreat and immediately tell everyone they know about how God changed their lives. Others need "baby steps" to help them become more confident. They all need help to learn the basic elements of the kerygma and how to share that with others, using their own witness so that it doesn't feel like a memorized speech but a sharing from the heart. They also need to have confidence that the Holy Spirit can use them, even with all their faults, to change the lives of others.

I love what Saint Paul wrote in the beginning of his letter to the Romans: "For I am not ashamed of the gospel. It is the power of God for the salvation of everyone who believes" (Rom 1:16). "We" are not the power of God; the Gospel is. We just have to share it! This is why we need to return to the Gospel message, over and over, lest we fall into the prideful trap of thinking that people's lives can change because we are such great people, or that we have done anything to deserve God's grace or his love. "For by grace you have been saved through faith, and this is not from you; it is the gift of God; it is not from works, so no one may boast" (Eph 2:8–9).

My favorite description of evangelization is "one beggar telling another beggar where to find bread." Or, as in the example of John chapter 4, "where to find living water." We do not need to dress up or be clever with the kerygma — no one could possibly make it more attractive than it already is. We just need to share this Gospel with others, just as we share our lives.

Jesus takes care of the rest.

Saint Photini, pray for us!

Questions for Reflection and Discussion

- The Spirit moves in our heart every time that we hear the kerygma explained or proclaimed. On a personal level, how did the Spirit speak to your heart through this chapter?
- Of the three elements of the kerygma that Pope Francis proposed (Jesus loves you, Jesus saves you, Jesus is with you), which one do you find the easiest to share? Which is the most difficult?
- What did you think about how heaven and hell were articulated in this chapter? What did you think about the description of the Church?
- What practical ideas come to mind on how to proclaim the kerygma "over and over" in the various activities that you do with teenagers?

An Exercise

The kerygma has to come from the heart. One can't understand, "Jesus loves you, he gave his life to save you …" unless a person shares, "Jesus loves *me*, he gave his life to save *me* … and he is with you, too." In about two hundred to four hundred words (two or three minutes of speech), briefly try to incorporate your personal witness into the kerygma, with an invitation at the end. This isn't creating a script to memorize. It's an exercise in blending the main points of the Good News with how that has changed our lives. Exercises such as this are a great way to "always be ready to give an explanation to anyone who asks you for a reason for your hope" (1 Pt 3:15). If you are doing this with a group, set aside some time to share your proclamations of the kerygma with each other.

If it helps, here is how I would do that (in about 240 words):

> I didn't have the most pleasant childhood. Not physically abused or anything, but lots of loneliness and despair. Then in high school I met some people who really loved

Jesus, and they loved me, too. I started getting more involved in Church and reading the Bible. I started to go to reconciliation on a more regular basis, and even go to Mass on days other than Sunday. Through all of that, I realized that the God of the Universe loved me so much that he became a baby in a stable and died on a cross so I could be with him forever. Jesus loved *me*. Jesus died on the cross to save *me*. And now he is with me everywhere I go, every moment of the day. It might sound crazy, but he is my friend. With the help of his Spirit, I try to be more like him: more loving, caring, giving. He has given me a peace that the world can never give. Jesus wants that for you, too. He didn't just die for me, he died for *us*. He is madly in love with *you* and wants you to know that he is with you, right here, right now. No sin can get in the way of his love; he destroyed sin on the cross. Jesus wants you to experience his mercy and his presence in this life and the life to come.

6
The Well and the Road

In June of 2024, the US bishops approved a new document entitled *Listen, Teach, Send: A National Pastoral Framework for Ministries with Youth and Young Adults*. It uses the story of the two disciples on the road to Emmaus as a model for ministry with youths (*A Vision of Youth Ministry* and *Christus Vivit* did this, too). Take a moment to pray with this Scripture. It is in Luke 24:13–35.

— *Insert your prayerful reading here* —

Listen, Teach, Send highlights three essential moments within that story that can serve as a model for ministry with youths:

> A transformation, or *metanoia*, can take place because Jesus first listens, teaches, then sends them. The Church, following Christ's example, is called to do the same: to *listen* to young people, to *teach* them the Gospel, and to *send* them forth into the world, alive in the

> Spirit. This "listen-teach-send" triptych is a framework to further develop concrete ministerial plans. Just as "Jesus himself drew near and walked with them … while they were conversing and debating" (Lk 23:15), Christ draws near to us once more, as we ourselves continue to converse and discern the best practices and latest trends about young people. His constant and eternal presence, made manifest in the Word of God and the Eucharist, ceaselessly aids us as we embark upon a journey in the company of the young, with hopeful hearts. The Holy Spirit, the divine protagonist active in our world today, strengthens and moves us toward the Church's preeminent mission of evangelization, offering us motivation to move forward in hope.

Using the "triptych" of *listen, teach*, and *send*, we can see the parallels of this method in what we read from the fourth chapter of John.

John 4	**Luke 24**
Listen	
He had to pass through Samaria. … Jesus, tired from his journey, sat down there at the well (4, 6).	Now that very day two of them were going to a village seven miles from Jerusalem called Emmaus. … And it happened that while they were conversing and debating, Jesus himself drew near and walked with them (13, 15).

<table>
<tr><td>Jesus said to her, “Give me a drink” (7).</td><td>He asked them, “What are you discussing as you walk along?” (17).</td></tr>
<tr><td>“How can you, a Jew, ask me, a Samaritan woman, for a drink?” (9).</td><td>“Are you the only visitor to Jerusalem who does not know of the things that have taken place there in these days?” (18).</td></tr>
<tr><td>“Sir, give me this water, so that I may not be thirsty or have to keep coming here to draw water” (15).</td><td>“But we were hoping that he would be the one to redeem Israel” (21).</td></tr>
<tr><td colspan="2" align="center">Teach</td></tr>
<tr><td>“You people worship what you do not understand; we worship what we understand, because salvation is from the Jews. But the hour is coming, and is now here, when true worshipers will worship the Father in Spirit and truth” (22–23).</td><td>And he said to them, “Oh, how foolish you are! How slow of heart to believe all that the prophets spoke! Was it not necessary that the Messiah should suffer these things and enter into his glory?” Then beginning with Moses and all the prophets, he interpreted to them what referred to him in all the scriptures (25–27).</td></tr>
<tr><td>The woman said to him, “I know that the Messiah is coming, the one called the Anointed; when he comes, he will tell us everything.” Jesus said to her, “I am he, the one who is speaking with you” (25–26).</td><td>And it happened that, while he was with them at table, he took bread, said the blessing, broke it, and gave it to them. With that their eyes were opened and they recognized him (30–31).</td></tr>
</table>

Send	
The woman left her water jar and went into the town and said to the people, "Come see a man who told me everything I have done. Could he possibly be the Messiah?" … Many of the Samaritans of that town began to believe in him because of the word of the woman who testified (28–29, 39).	So they set out at once and returned to Jerusalem where they found gathered together the eleven and those with them. … Then the two recounted what had taken place on the way and how he was made known to them in the breaking of the bread (33, 35).

Different People, Same Method

Those whom Jesus encountered in these stories could not have been more disparate. Photini was a Samaritan woman who met Jesus for the first time; Cleopas and the other disciple on the road to Emmaus were Jewish men who had been disciples of Jesus for years but didn't fully understand who he was. The teenagers we minister with can be vastly different, too. In every parish and Catholic school we find young people at various stages on their journey of faith.

Though teenagers will be different, the method is the same. Ministry begins by going where they are, even if that means going to "pagan territory" or walking in the wrong direction. This is where we patiently wait and show that we want to "listen" to their felt needs, experiences, frustrations, and questions.

We "teach" what Jesus taught — even the things that are challenging to hear. We also teach the *way* that Jesus taught. He practiced what he preached. He was the model of love and compassion. Jesus rarely lectured. His method of teaching was primarily to ask questions, use parables, invite them to new experiences, and help them to "rethink" what they thought that they knew, so as to recognize the truth themselves.

Though neither Photini nor the two disciples were specifically "sent" by Jesus to share him with others, it was the natural thing to do! This is our desire for young people: that they not only be recipients of the Gospel message but active witnesses, through words and deeds, that Jesus Christ is alive and in their midst. Our "send" is not sending them off on their own, waving goodbye and saying, "Have fun storming the castle!" It is inviting them to be part of a community of missionary disciples who continue to bring the saving message of Jesus Christ to the world. We don't say, "Go away" but instead say, "Join us!"

THIS IS OUR DESIRE FOR YOUNG PEOPLE: THAT THEY NOT ONLY BE RECIPIENTS OF THE GOSPEL MESSAGE BUT ACTIVE WITNESSES, THROUGH WORDS AND DEEDS, THAT JESUS CHRIST IS ALIVE AND IN THEIR MIDST.

This process is not just linear but cyclical. It is well known that Jesus sent out the apostles at the end of the Gospel, but what is sometimes overlooked is that he sent them out at least a couple of times before that: "So [the apostles] went off and preached repentance. They drove out many demons, and they anointed with oil many who were sick and cured them" (Mk 6:12–13). In our ministry with teens, we listen a little, teach a little, and send a little, so that we can listen more, teach more, and send more. Like any relationship, it grows step by step, slow and in stages. This is why young people need many mentors for the journey.

I would also add that this applies to us as well. To state the obvious, we are not Jesus. We do not have exclusive rights to the

Holy Spirit. Recall the reciprocal nature of youth ministry described at the beginning of the book: The goal of youth ministry is a sharing of gifts between youths and adults so that we can be one Body in Christ. We must be open to the gifts of the Spirit that they can share with us. I love this quote from Pope Francis:

> To be credible to young people, there are times when she needs to regain her humility and simply listen, recognizing that what others have to say can provide some light to help her better understand the Gospel. A Church always on the defensive, which loses her humility and stops listening to others, which leaves no room for questions, loses her youth and turns into a museum. How, then, will she be able to respond to the dreams of young people? Even if she possesses the truth of the Gospel, this does not mean that she has completely understood it; rather, she is called to keep growing in her grasp of that inexhaustible treasure. (*Christus Vivit*, 41)

I have been amazed at the profound insights of faith that teens have had over the years. I have been humbled by their zeal to share the Gospel and do works of mercy. Yes, I have been involved with ministries that have listened to them, taught them, and sent them. But I have been truly blessed for the times that they listened to me, taught me, and even sent me to places that I wouldn't gone without them!

Sharing the Faith through Friendship

Though I love the simplicity of "listen, teach, send," there is always the danger (as the document itself warns against) of those terms being misunderstood. As a father, I've had moments when my kids did something wrong, so I *listened* to their explanation, *taught* what they should have done, and *sent* them to their room as punishment. That is obviously not what we are supposed to do in ministry with youths! But sadly, it is the way that many adults approach teenagers.

"Listen, teach, send" is only effective in the context of friendships. Pope Francis loves to use the word *accompaniment* when talking about ministry with young people. Like any word or phrase, it can lose its meaning when it gets overused, and such terms naturally have a shelf-life until something newer comes along. What I love about *accompaniment* is its literal meaning. It comes from the Latin phrase *ad cum panis*, which means "to share bread with." The story of Jesus encountering two disciples on the road to Emmaus is the ultimate "accompaniment" story because it concludes with "He was made known to them in the breaking of the bread" (Lk 24:35). The process that leads to that revelation — listen, teach, and send — is all part of what is meant by the word *accompaniment*.

In the next part of the book, I will try to break down what accompaniment is (and isn't), and how we can share the Faith with teenagers by sharing our lives.

Questions for Reflection and Discussion

- When you read Luke 24:13–35, what other insights did you gain on how we might pass the Faith on to teenagers?
- Reread the story, but this time imagine yourself as one of the disciples on the road and a teenager as the other. How does that change your perspective on ministry?
- What has God revealed to you through the teenagers you minister with? How have they listened, taught, and sent you?

Part 2

With Our Lives

7
The Holy Ground of Adolescence

The saints are my friends. Some are friends because I have so much in common with them. For example, I love Saint Lawrence because he was a deacon and was funny — and I'd like to think that I'm a funny deacon, too.

With others it is more like "opposites attract." That's my relationship with José Sánchez del Rio. I don't want to portray myself as a wimp, but I am far more comfortable on a stage than I would be on the battlefield. José was a "man's man," willing to fight any giant for what was right and unwilling to back down from his beliefs for any reason. When the government tried to exterminate his religion, he joined the rebellion. When the battle was lost and his general was about to be captured, José gave his vehicle to the general so that he could escape, leaving himself to be captured. The enemy tried to starve and torture José, telling him that they'd let him go if he denied his faith. He steadfastly refused, even when his crying mother begged him to do as they asked!

Then came the death march. They cut the soles off José's feet and forced him to walk a rough-hewn path. With every painful step he forgave his persecutors and praised God. When they got to his freshly dug grave, they gave José one last chance for life, if only he would curse God. He bent down and made the Sign of the Cross on the ground with his own blood. Then he looked up, faced the soldiers, and proudly yelled in his native language, "Long live Christ the King!" It took two shots to take his life and drop his body into the grave.

St. José Sánchez del Rio was only fourteen years old. I am in no way being facetious when I say that when I grow up, I want to be a man like him.

Hidden Saints

Another friend of mine is St. Maria Goretti. At the age of eleven, she refused to let a man rape her, not only to preserve her own innocence but because she was worried that he might go to hell if he did so. He killed her instead. While he was in prison for his crime, Maria came to him in a vision and let him know that he was forgiven. He immediately converted to the Faith. When released from prison after twenty-eight years, he went to Maria's family and begged for forgiveness, then spent the rest of his life in prayer and penance as a gardener for a monastery.

The stories of teenage saints are tragic, from a worldly perspective, because they end with the death of a young person. The horrific manner of their deaths brings forth the beauty of their faith in a way that might not have been seen otherwise. Had they lived in a different time and place, those tragic things might not have happened to them. That would not have made them less holy — only more hidden.

Think of Bl. Carlo Acutis. His early death from cancer is not what made him holy. It was the devotion of his life, his love of the Eucharist and the Blessed Mother. His death simply revealed what was hidden: a teenage saint in our midst.

In my years of ministry with teenagers, I have met many hidden saints like these. Teenagers who I'm confident would face such trials bravely if they had to. Such lives are not common, but they are also not unique. You have to rise above the negativity that many adults have about teenagers and see the holiness that they have, or at least the potential for it.

YOU HAVE TO RISE ABOVE THE NEGATIVITY THAT MANY ADULTS HAVE ABOUT TEENAGERS AND SEE THE HOLINESS THAT THEY HAVE, OR AT LEAST THE POTENTIAL FOR IT.

In *Christus Vivit,* Pope Francis writes:

> We adults can often be tempted to list all the problems and failings of today's young people. Perhaps some will find it praiseworthy that we seem so expert in discerning difficulties and dangers. But what would be the result of such an attitude? Greater distance, less closeness, less mutual assistance.
>
> Anyone called to be a parent, pastor or guide to young people must have the farsightedness to appreciate the little flame that continues to burn, the fragile reed that is shaken but not broken (see Is 42:3). The ability to discern pathways where others only see walls, to recognize potential where others see only peril. That is how God the Father see [*sic*] things; he knows how to cherish and nurture the seeds of goodness sown in the hearts of the young. Each young person's heart should thus be considered "holy ground", a bearer of seeds of

> divine life, before which we must "take off our shoes" in order to draw near and enter more deeply into the Mystery. (66–67)

Finding Jesus in the Temple

The thirty years that passed between the birth of Jesus and the start of his public ministry are known as the "hidden life of Jesus." The Gospels don't provide any stories of what happened between the Holy Family's arrival in Nazareth and Jesus' appearance at the Jordan River — except for one. When Jesus was an adolescent.

Let's take a moment to reflect on this story. This is what we meditate upon in the Rosary's fifth Joyful Mystery, the Finding of Jesus in the Temple. Prayerfully read it. Imagine what Jesus looked like as a twelve-year-old and what you would have seen and heard if you had been in the Temple that day:

> Each year his parents went to Jerusalem for the feast of Passover, and when he was twelve years old, they went up according to festival custom. After they had completed its days, as they were returning, the boy Jesus remained behind in Jerusalem, but his parents did not know it. Thinking that he was in the caravan, they journeyed for a day and looked for him among their relatives and acquaintances, but not finding him, they returned to Jerusalem to look for him. After three days they found him in the temple, sitting in the midst of the teachers, listening to them and asking them questions, and all who heard him were astounded at his understanding and his answers. When his parents saw him, they were astonished, and his mother said to him, "Son, why have you done this to us? Your father and I have been looking for you with great anxiety." And he said

> to them, "Why were you looking for me? Did you not know that I must be in my Father's house?" But they did not understand what he said to them. He went down with them and came to Nazareth, and was obedient to them; and his mother kept all these things in her heart. And Jesus advanced [in] wisdom and age and favor before God and man. (Luke 2:41–52)

The first question that you're likely to ask when reading the passage is "How did they lose Jesus?" Pope Francis offers a beautiful insight:

> "Jesus did not grow up in a narrow and stifling relationship with Mary and Joseph, but readily interacted with the wider family, the relatives of his parents and their friends." Hence we can understand why, when he returned from his pilgrimage to Jerusalem, his parents readily thought that, as a twelve-year-old boy (cf. Lk 2:42), he was wandering freely among the crowd, even though they did not see him for an entire day: "supposing him to be in the group of travellers, they went a day's journey" (Lk 2:44). Surely, they assumed, Jesus was there, mingling with the others, joking with other young people, listening to the adults tell stories and sharing the joys and sorrows of the group (*Christus Vivit,* 29).

Francis imagines the teenage Jesus as a sociable kid who often spent time with others. So, it was natural for his parents to assume that he was somewhere in the caravan of people who traveled together from Nazareth to Jerusalem and back. The men usually walked in one group, and the women and children in another, so it was only at the end of the day that they got together and realized that Jesus wasn't there. Since it was dangerous to travel at night, they had to wait for the sun to rise and spend another day making it back to Jerusalem. Then, on the third day, when they are visiting all their friends and relatives in search of their son, they find him in the Temple.

Though many paintings of this moment show a young boy teaching very impressed older people, the Bible says that he was "sitting in the midst of the teachers, listening to them and asking them questions" (Lk 2:46). Oh, the humility of God! The Incarnate Word is coming to adults with questions about the Faith. But why?

Jesus was fully God and fully human, like us in all things except for sin. He had a human intellect and human will, just as he had a divine intellect and a divine will. There are numerous times when Scripture shows that Jesus didn't "cheat" the human experience by drawing upon his divine omnipotence. He allowed his human brain to develop and mature as anyone else's would. As a baby, he didn't immediately speak all the languages of the world. Instead, he learned to speak Hebrew one syllable at a time, probably messing some up as he did. Jesus didn't jump out of the cradle as a child and run full speed. First he crawled, then he walked, and he likely fell a few times along the way. Just like we did.

Jesus experienced adolescence. He felt growing pains. He got clumsy and awkward. Jesus likely found himself energized in the evening and exhausted in the morning, as many teenagers do. Jesus even allowed himself to *think* like a teenager. Listen to his response to Mary's question:

> His mother said to him, "Son, why have you done this to us? Your father and I have been looking for you with great anxiety." And he said to them, "Why were you looking for me? Did you not know that I must be in my Father's house?" But they did not understand what he said to them. (Luke 2:48–50)

One of the challenges within an adolescent's brain is the lack of ability to foresee consequences to their actions. When a young teenager does something foolish or reckless, adults immediately ask, "*What were you thinking?*" It is an unfair question to an adolescent whose brain has not yet fully developed the ability to determine cause and effect. They *were* thinking, but only about the moment that they were in, not about what would happen next.

"Why were you looking for me?" (Lk 2:49) is such an adolescent thing to say, isn't it? The twelve-year-old Jesus implies that this isn't his problem, it is theirs. And though their son was without sin, Mary and Joseph got to experience what every parent of a teenager experiences: "They did not understand what he said to them" (2:50). Even in a family made up of the Incarnate Word, the Immaculate Conception, and the Patron Saint of the Universal Church, the adolescence of Jesus brought with it confusion, miscommunication, and anxiety. No wonder adolescence has wreaked such havoc on sinful families … like mine!

The story concludes by saying that Jesus "went down with them and came to Nazareth, and was obedient to them" (Lk 2:51), meaning that he did what they said, even if he didn't want to. Young people are often filled with zeal and want to take on the world, even if they aren't ready to do so. This seemed to be the case with Jesus. He wanted to begin his public ministry right then and there. His mother had the wisdom to temper (but not squash) that enthusiasm by saying, "Not yet." So, he was obedient and patiently waited for the right time. How beautiful it is that thirty years later, Jesus' first public miracle occurred only after his mother told him to do it (see Jn 2:1–11, the Wedding at Cana).

Loving the Adolescent Jesus

We often imagine Jesus at different stages of his life: as a baby in Bethlehem, as a teacher during the Sermon on the Mount, tortured and crucified in Jerusalem, victorious before the empty tomb, or seated on a throne of glory in heaven. How often do we think and meditate about Jesus as a teenager? If the paintings created by artists are any indication, not much.

WHEN WE SEE JESUS AS A TEENAGER, WE CAN SEE JESUS IN TEENAGERS, AND WE CAN HELP TEENS SEE JESUS IN THEMSELVES.

I would encourage you to have a relationship with the adolescent Jesus. Just as you might prayerfully imagine what it would be like to hold Jesus as an infant or to kneel before him at the foot of the cross when he was an adult, make praying to the adolescent Jesus a part of your spiritual life. He was a fun kid to be around. I find that the more that we can see Jesus *as* a teen, the more that we can recognize Jesus *in* the teens we minister with. Jesus is present in their high school, as are teens like José, Maria, and Carlos. They are little flames that need to be cherished and nurtured, "holy ground" wherein we can "enter more deeply into the Mystery" (*Christus Vivit*, 67).

When we see Jesus as a teenager, we can see Jesus *in* teenagers, and we can help teens see Jesus in themselves, because each of them is "a bearer of seeds of divine life."

St. José Sánchez del Rio, *pray for us*!

St. Maria Goretti, *pray for us*!

Bl. Carlo Acutis, *pray for us*!

Jesus Christ, who became an adolescent for us, *have mercy on us*!

Questions for Reflection and Discussion

- Reread the quote from *Christus Vivit* 67: "Each

young person's heart should thus be considered 'holy ground.'" What stood out to you?

- What were some insights that you received when prayerfully reading Luke 2:41–52?
- How did Pope Francis's insights on Jesus as an adolescent give you deeper understanding of that passage?
- How did prayerfully imagining Jesus as an adolescent change your perspective of Jesus and/or teenagers?

8
Be Not Afraid!

Pope St. Paul VI wrote: "Above all the Gospel must be proclaimed by witness. … Nevertheless this always remains insufficient, because even the finest witness will prove ineffective in the long run if it is not explained, justified … and made explicit by a clear and unequivocal proclamation of the Lord Jesus" (*Evangelii Nuntiandi*, 21–22). When I present that quote in the many workshops I give, nobody argues with me. Heads nod. People murmur their agreement.

"So," I ask, "who then is the best person to proclaim the Gospel?" The answers range from how the bishop should be bolder, priests should have better homilies, religion teachers should be less boring, and parents should do their job and talk about the Faith with their kids. None of these answers are bad — there is truth in all of them. But they can also be summed up as, "Somebody other than me."

The correct answer is *you* — the one who accompanies, the one who has earned their trust, the one with whom they feel safe to talk.

If you are freaking out about that, you are in good company. Consider Moses' first reaction when the Lord said that *he* would lead the Hebrews out of Egypt:

> Moses, however, said to the LORD, "If you please, my Lord, I have never been eloquent, neither in the past nor now that you have spoken to your servant; but I am slow of speech and tongue." The LORD said to him: Who gives one person speech? Who makes another mute or deaf, seeing or blind? Is it not I, the LORD? Now go, I will assist you in speaking and teach you what you are to say. But he said, "If you please, my Lord, send someone else!" (Exodus 4:10–13).

It is tempting to hire a professional conference speaker to come speak to your youths about the Gospel message, or bring teens to an event that has great preaching. I'm not suggesting to not do that. As a conference speaker myself, I absolutely love the opportunity to use my talents on stage to share the Good News. So yes, bring teens to a conference, a camp, or a retreat where they can hear inspiring talks from people who are really good at giving them.

But remember that teens (honestly, most people) are more interested in *who* is talking than *what* is being said. You might not have the engaging voice, dramatic stories, or polished presentation of people who do it for a living, but that's not the point. Your proclamation of Jesus will have a more profound impact just because it is *you* who are sharing it.

Also, you can share it in the right place at the right moment in the context of that teenager's life. When I'm hired to speak somewhere, I talk at 7:20 p.m. because it's on the schedule, whether the audience is spiritually ready or not. You, however, get to be on the Spirit's schedule, the perfect timing that only he can provide.

The kerygma should be preached from the pulpit. It must be said in sacramental preparation. It must be communicated in catechesis. These places are all important. We need to hear it over and over, and the liturgical cycle gives us the opportunity to do that every year. But you, who are willing to share your life with teens, are in a special and unique place to share the Gospel in a powerful, life-changing way. You don't need to be a theologian to do it. It's not so much about being articulate as authentic. Someone else might say it better, but nobody can share it like you can. You can look a teenager in the eye and say, "Jesus has changed my life, and he can change yours, too." Remember that "the holy Spirit will teach you at that moment what you should say" (Lk 12:12). So be not afraid!

> YOU, WHO ARE WILLING TO SHARE YOUR LIFE WITH TEENS, ARE IN A SPECIAL AND UNIQUE PLACE TO SHARE THE GOSPEL IN A POWERFUL, LIFE-CHANGING WAY.

The "Under-Qualified"

If this call to preach the Gospel intimidates you, then *good*. Here is the irony: Feeling overwhelmed and under-qualified to do relational ministry with youths is not an obstacle. It is actually a prerequisite.

Scripture is filled with stories of the under-qualified who are called. One of my favorites in the Old Testament is about Gideon. The Lord told Gideon that he would use him to overthrow the Midianites, who were oppressing his people. So, Gideon gathered an army of thirty-two thousand soldiers. The army of Midian was so large that it couldn't be counted, "for they were as many as the sands on the seashore" (Jgs 7:12). The Israelites were seriously outnumbered. So, imagine Gideon's surprise when the Lord told him, "You have too many soldiers with you for me to deliver Midian into their power, lest Israel vaunt itself against me and say, 'My own power saved me'" (7:2).

Think about that for a second. God didn't want the Israelite army to be *too* strong, lest they convince themselves that they could win by their own power.

It gets even crazier. When Gideon shrank the army to ten thousand, just one third of the previous size, the Lord said, "There are still too many soldiers" (7:4). What?!? So, God told Gideon to take the army to a river and watch how the soldiers drank. The ones who knelt down and drank the water with a cupped hand were put in one group. The ones who went into the water face first and lapped it up with their tongues were in another. 9,700 soldiers drank water the more civilized way. The other three hundred soldiers acted like thirsty dogs.

Guess which ones the Lord chose to go into battle?

You can also probably guess who won.

Look at the "army" that the world has assembled to attract the hearts of teenagers: gorgeous movie stars, talented musicians, superstar athletes, cutting-edge technologies, beautiful (and often scandalous) fashion … the list goes on. An American teenager is considered to be the greatest commodity on the planet, and the rest of the world falls over itself to get their attention. And, of course, their *money*.

Compare this to the kind of people who show up at a leadership meeting for youth ministry at a parish or Catholic high school. No offense, but we're not winning any beauty pageants. We aren't especially attractive, athletic, or talented. Some of us are a little awkward, others are decidedly "uncool." There are also not that many of us. Oh, and did I mention that we are woefully underfunded?

Many adults feel that they don't have the skills, knowledge, "cool factor," or ability to do ministry with teenagers. Let's face it, teenagers can be very intimidating. They are also usually skeptical of what adults want from them. From their perspective, most teens view adults as people who try to get them to do what they don't want to do, whether that be household chores (parents), studying (teachers), practicing (coaches), or obeying laws that they don't agree with (police). They assume that the main job of a youth minister is to be a "religious enforcer," which isn't a great way to start a relationship. So yes, building relationships with teens can be a difficult, uphill battle. It is natural that any adult might not feel up to the task. Though the odds are clearly stacked against us, the stories in Scripture and the lives of the saints tell us time and time again that "for God all things are possible" (Mt 19:26).

Imitators of Jesus

As Saint Paul was trying to explain to the Church in Corinth how to follow the ways of Jesus, he wrote, "Be imitators of me, as I am of Christ" (1 Cor 11:1). Think about how bold that statement is. How many of you would stand up in front of a group of people and say, "You be like me, I'll be like Christ, and everything will be fine." *Yeah, right.*

Here's the thing: Saint Paul was just acknowledging what people already thought. When we publicly declare ourselves to be Catholic, people look at our behavior and think, "Well, that's what Catholics do." That can be good! That can be bad. And sometimes, *really* bad.

Scandal gets more attention than sanctity. How many people have left the Catholic Church (or would not even consider joining) because of the sexual scandal caused by some of her clergy? There are many, many "counter-witnesses" to what it means to be Catholic in our culture today. The most elegant and inspiring talk about Catholicism will make no difference if people think that the one giving the message is a fraud. The message is only as credible as the messenger.

It is only through the witness of believers that the Faith can be passed on. Pope St. John Paul II wrote, "People today put more trust in witnesses than in teachers, in experience than in teaching, and in life and action than in theories. The witness of a Christian life is the first and irreplaceable form of mission. … The missionary who, despite all his or her human limitations and defects, lives a simple life, taking Christ as the model, is a sign of God and of transcendent realities" (*Redemptoris Missio*, 42). I always take comfort in the phrase, "despite all his or her human limitations and defects." If witnessing to the Faith required someone to be perfect, then Christianity would have never made it out of the first century!

There were a lot of things that Saint Paul could have bragged about. Personally, I found the time when he raised someone from the dead pretty impressive (see Acts 20:10–11). I would have *definitely* included that in my bio. However, when he complained to the Lord about "a thorn in the flesh," Jesus said to him, "My grace is sufficient for you, for power is made perfect in weakness." So Paul decided, "I will rather boast most gladly of my weaknesses, in order that the power of Christ may dwell with me" (2 Cor 12:6, 9).

It goes against our nature to "boast" of our weaknesses. Nobody puts their ugly pictures on social media; we only want people to see our best side. If you saw me speaking in front of a group of people, you'd be surprised how much time I took with my hair to make it look like I hadn't spent much time on my hair.

We naturally want to give a great "spiritual" appearance, too. We can try to look like the "super-Catholic" who never misses daily Mass or prayer time, never has any doubts, always does the right thing, and knows all the answers. Not only is that not realistic, it isn't attractive. I've talked to many young people who get discouraged by speakers who seem to have no faults or struggles in faith. They think, "Well, that's great for you, but what about me? I'm a mess!" Impressing someone with the Faith is not the same as imparting it.

The life of a disciple is that of a *forgiven sinner*. Jesus has changed our life! We are confident that "the one who began a good work in you will continue to complete it" (Phil 1:6), but we are still works in progress. We need to admit that more, especially to young people.

An important note: Publicly admitting that we are sinners is not the same as publicly confessing our sin. Again, Saint Paul gives us another great example to imitate: "For I do not do the good I want, but I do the evil I do not want" (Rom 7:19). He had no problem saying that he still sinned, that he was weak, and that he had a "thorn in the flesh." But what exactly was that "thorn"? What particular sins did he wrestle with? *We have no idea*. That was between him and God. What mattered is that he said enough for us to know that he was a work in progress, too. Then he put the focus back on Jesus.

I think that Pope Francis said it perfectly, and it's worth taking some time to reflect on these words:

> All of us are called to offer others an explicit witness to the saving love of the Lord, who despite our imperfections offers us his closeness, his word and his strength, and gives meaning to our lives. In your heart you know that it is not the same to live without him; what you have come to realize, what has helped you to live and given you hope, is what you also need to communicate to others. Our falling short of perfection should be no excuse; on the contrary, mission is a constant stimulus not to remain mired in mediocrity but to continue growing.

> The witness of faith that each Christian is called to offer leads us to say with Saint Paul: "Not that I have already obtained this, or am already perfect; but I press on to make it my own, because Christ Jesus has made me his own." (*Evangelii Gaudium,* 121)

Ven. Jan Tyranowski

One great example of a seemingly "unqualified" person is Ven. Jan Tyranowski. Born at the start of the twentieth century in Krakow, Poland, Jan (pronounced *yahn* — it is Polish for "John") was described as a loner and was fascinated by science. He also suffered from health issues that caused him to lose his job as an accountant and take up tailoring with his father. He lived in a small apartment in Krakow by himself.

When he was thirty-five years old, he heard a homily at Mass that changed his life. "It is not difficult to be a saint," the priest said. As a layperson, Jan had thought that holiness was for priests and religious, not tailors! This message spoke to his heart. He began to devote himself to prayer and to reading books from the saints, especially St. John of the Cross.

This was a difficult time in Poland, as many feared the growing power of Nazi Germany. When Jan was thirty-nine, the Germans invaded. The following year, more than half of the clergy of Poland had been deported. The pastor at his parish (fearing that he would be deported soon) asked Jan if he would take over ministry for the young men in the parish. That wasn't something that Jan had been involved with before, but he said that he'd try.

Jan had a high-pitched voice and felt awkward in front of people. He did not make a good first impression. One of the boys, Mieczyslaw, was concerned that he might be a Gestapo agent. Another boy, Karol, thought that he was unbearable. Jan slowly won them over with his sincerity and constant presence. When Karol's father died a year later, Jan was there to comfort him and help him through that loss. Over his seven years of ministry, Jan faithfully led hundreds of young men (in their teens and twenties) in meetings where they prayed the Rosary and discussed the Faith. A number of them became priests and religious, including Karol and Mieczyslaw, both of whom credited him for helping them discern their vocation. Though seriously ill, Jan got to see Karol's ordination. He died a year later at the age of forty-seven.

Karol, if you didn't know, eventually became pope and took the name John Paul II. He declared Jan a Servant of God in 1997, and Pope Francis elevated Jan to Venerable in 2017.

Not bad for a tailor!

Just as I believe that every parish has hidden teenage saints like José, Maria, and Carlo, I believe that parishes are also filled with loving adults like Jan Tyranowski — simple people who say yes even though they feel overwhelmed and under-qualified. Men and women who are present to young people, listen to their stories, point out their gifts, accompany them on their journeys, comfort them in trials, encourage them to holiness, and share with them the "reason for your hope" (1 Pt 3:15), Jesus Christ.

Christ-like Humility

We see in Jan Tyranowski many of the qualities that Pope Francis listed were important for those who accompany the young:

> A faithful Christian who engages with the Church and the world; someone who constantly seeks holiness; someone who is a confidant without judging. Similarly, someone who actively listens to the needs of young people and responds in kind; someone deeply loving and self-aware; someone who recognizes his or her limits and knows the joys and sorrows of the spiritual journey. An especially important quality in mentors is the acknowledgement of their own humanity — the fact that

> they are human beings who make mistakes: not perfect people but forgiven sinners. (*Christus Vivit*, 246)

Humility is an important theme that runs through many of those qualities: the humility to constantly seek God, the humility to acknowledge one's own sinfulness, and the humility to not judge others but listen with an empathic heart.

CHRIST-LIKE HUMILITY LEADS US TO "TAKE OFF OUR SHOES" BEFORE THE SACREDNESS OF THE YOUNG AND SERVE THEM AS JESUS WOULD.

St. John the Baptist, upon observing Jesus begin his public ministry and realizing that his own prophetic efforts would need to make way for the Lord's work, said "He must increase; I must decrease" (Jn 3:30). Ministries with both youths and young adults should be inspired by this same humility; they should not be "personality-driven." When a cult of celebrity takes over, one might think that they are the one to whom young people are flocking, or that they are the singular keepers of the faith. Nothing could be further from the truth!

One of the most profound actions of Jesus was when he took off his outer garments and washed the feet of the apostles — even the feet of the one who was about to betray him. Jesus said, "I am among you as the one who serves" (Lk 22:27). Christ-like humility leads us to "take off our shoes" before the sacredness of the young and serve them as Jesus would. Francis wrote, "Let us also keep in mind that Jesus had no use for adults who looked down on the young or lorded it over them" (*Christus Vivit*, 14). We must always remember that the word *ministry* has *minus* in it. If the Lord of Lords did not "lord" his authority over his followers, how can anyone else?

Jesus Is Their Answer

I had the wonderful experience of taking fifty teenagers to World Youth Day in Rome in the year 2000. Sitting in a crowd of over a million young people from around the world, Pope St. John Paul II said:

> It is Jesus in fact that you seek when you dream of happiness; he is waiting for you when nothing else you find satisfies you. … It is Jesus who stirs in you the desire to do something great with your lives, the will to follow an ideal, the refusal to allow yourselves to be grounded down by mediocrity, the courage to commit yourselves humbly and patiently to improving yourselves and society, making the world more human and more fraternal.

It is Jesus that they seek. We who minister with youths must be convicted of that in our hearts. Jesus is not *an* option. He is *the* option. Jesus is the way, the truth, and the life. Jesus came "so that they might have life and have it more abundantly" (Jn 10:10). And he meant it when he said, "Behold, I am with you always" (Mt 28:20).

Jesus told us, "As I have loved you, so you also should love one another" (Jn 13:34). That is the love that we share with teenagers. It is real. It is authentic. It is greater than anything else that the world can offer. It can't be replicated at a concert or replaced by an iPhone. It is a love that invites teenagers into a community, a family of faith. At the center of that family is Jesus himself, risen from the dead and alive in our midst.

"Without me you can do nothing" (Jn 15:5), but with him, "all things are possible" (Mt 19:26). It is a clichéd phrase but it is worth repeating: God does not call the qualified, he qualifies the called.

So, if you are called, then "do not be afraid" (Mt 14:27, and a few hundred other places in Scripture) to say *yes*. If you have years of experience, remember to "Trust in the LORD with all your heart, / on your own intelligence do not rely" (Prv 3:5). "The one who calls you is faithful, and he will also accomplish it" (1 Thes 5:24), just like he did in Jan's life and the lives of countless others.

It isn't about being good enough; it is about being *graced* enough. And God's graces are available to us all.

St. John Paul II, *pray for us*!

Ven. Jan Tyranowski, *pray for us*!

Questions for Reflection and Discussion

- When God called Moses, Moses gave him a list of excuses. What excuses or anxieties do you have that get in the way of ministering with youths?
- Reflect upon the quote from *Evangelii Gaudium*, 121 ("Our falling short of perfection should be no excuse ..."). How does that inspire you?
- Reflect upon the quote from *Christus Vivit*, 246 ("A faithful Christian who engages with the Church and the world ..."). Does that describe you? If not, which of those qualities do you feel that you need to work on?
- What in this chapter helped you to "be not afraid"?

Interlude: Another Dream

It was the Saturday night of the retreat. We had an open mic time for teens to share how the Lord had touched their life that weekend. A girl stood up, and I noticed that she was holding a folder.

"The Lord has changed my life this weekend," she began. There were many nods in the audience. Someone yelled, "Preach it, sister!" and a few kids laughed. She smiled and continued. "It was cool to hear how Jesus suffered and died for my sins, and the time of Eucharistic adoration happened like it usually does. But what really changed my life this weekend ... was *this*."

She reached into her folder and pulled out the flyer that I had designed for the retreat.

If I do say so myself, it was a pretty awesome flyer. I can't even estimate how many days I spent getting it just right. I even pushed the budget for a full-color print. But why was it in a folder?

"I put it in a folder so that it wouldn't get folded or wrinkled. Just look at it," she said with admiration, and as she held it up, I could hear gasps in the crowd. "Everything is perfectly balanced, and the font selection was on point."

"Do you really think so?" I asked aloud. Everyone turned to me. I hadn't meant to speak; it just came out. So I continued. "I was worried using the Impact font was a bit out of date."

"It wasn't," said a boy from the crowd. He held up his own flyer, which also was perfectly intact. "I thought it gave a retro vibe."

"What about the clip art?" I asked. "Having a person with huge eyes looking at the price was ..."

"It was me," said another girl, standing to face me. "When I saw how reasonable the price was for the weekend, my eyes got that huge with excitement." Even as she spoke, I saw her eyes get huge, just like the clip art that I used. She looked at me with those big eyes and whispered, "*This flyer read my soul.*"

All the teens were standing now, facing me, holding their flyers. "Thank you," they all said in unison, "for all the days you spent on this. There was nothing better you could have spent your time on."

It was overwhelming. I began to cry so hard that I couldn't see anything through the tears, and when I wiped my face to see, I realized that I was in my bed. I sat up and looked around. It was just a dream. A beautiful dream.

But something felt ... wrong. What was it? What was missing?

When I realized it, I fell back to my pillow with frustration.

"They didn't mention the T-shirts," I mumbled.

Ungrateful punks.

9
Come, Holy Spirit!

It is God's perfect plan to use imperfect people like us to share the Good News and give him glory. As Saint Paul reminded the Corinthians: "Consider your own calling, brothers. Not many of you were wise by human standards, not many were powerful, not many were of noble birth. Rather, God chose the foolish of the world to shame the wise, and God chose the weak of the world to shame the strong" (1 Cor 1:26–27).

We are not Jesus, but we are filled with the "Spirit of Jesus," one of the many titles in Scripture given to the Holy Spirit. The *Catechism* explains this beautifully: "When the Father sends his Word, he always sends his Breath. In their joint mission, the Son and the Holy Spirit are distinct but inseparable. To be sure, it is Christ who is seen, the visible image of the invisible God, but it is the Spirit who reveals him" (689). A word cannot be heard unless there is breath. This is why constantly praying, "Come, Holy Spirit" is the best thing that we can do while we are accompanying young people. You never know when a "Spirit moment" might happen.

I hope that I am not speaking too much in the abstract. I find it ironic that even Catholics who believe that a piece of bread is transformed into the Body and Blood of the King of the Universe can have a hard time believing that the Holy Spirit can speak through them. Why do we expect miracles in the Divine Liturgy but not in our daily lives?

Perhaps it is because we underestimate the sacramental graces that we have received through baptism and confirmation. The Greek word *Christos* (translated in English as "Christ") and the Hebrew word *Mashiach* (translated as "Messiah") both mean "the anointed one." *Anoint* has two meanings. The first is to smear or rub something, such as oil. The deeper meaning is to confer authority upon someone. In both baptism and confirmation, a person is anointed with holy oil (or chrism) to incorporate them into Christ who is priest, prophet, and king. Just as *Christ* means "anointed one," the word *Christian* literally means "little anointed one." Jesus is the Christ, and through baptism and confirmation, we become "little Christs," anointed with his power and authority through the Holy Spirit who dwells within us.

Ministry in the Spirit

When you become active in ministry, when "Come, Holy Spirit" becomes the mantra of your heart, you start to see miracles. I define *miracles* as divine, supernatural interventions in our daily lives. Some would like to narrow this definition by adding "that can't be explained by any other natural phenomena," which I think is silly. If I ask God for something, and then that thing happens, then God did it. We don't give him enough credit for everything that he does in our lives. There are no such things as coincidences in life or in ministry — just "God incidents."

It is the thing that you just "happened" to say, which was exactly what that young person needed to hear. It is the donation that just "happened" to be the exact right amount to cover the cost of the retreat. It is the parent who just "happened" to forget to pick up their teen on time, providing you and that teen a few minutes to have a life-changing conversation in the parking lot. Miracles, miracles, miracles.

I've seen "unexplainable" miracles as well, like physical healings or prophetic knowledge. Don't close your mind to the possibilities of what the Holy Spirit can and will do if he is given unfettered permission to work. "For the kingdom of God is not a matter of talk but of power" (1 Cor 4:20).

Ministry cannot happen without the power of the Holy Spirit. Jesus said that "when he comes, the Spirit of truth, he will guide you to all truth" (Jn 16:13) and "when he comes he will convict the world in regard to sin and righteousness and condemnation" (Jn 16:8). We can try to convince the mind, but only the Spirit can convict the heart. On my own (and at my best), I might get a teenager to think, "Bob makes some good points. He might be right." But with the Holy Spirit, the response can be "I know this in my heart to be true."

I'D RATHER BE ANOINTED THAN GOOD.

In my decades of ministry and my thousands of talks, I can say with certainty that I have never once changed the heart of one of my listeners. The Holy Spirit has. That's what he does. Me? I witness and proclaim the truth with creativity, clarity, and conviction. The Spirit of truth does the rest. He makes things happen even if the programming doesn't go as planned, the sound system doesn't work, or I give a bad talk. I strive for excellence in everything I do, but I'd rather be anointed than good.

The Other Voices

How does one hear the Holy Spirit? To begin, it is good to be aware that there are other voices that vie for our attention, pretending to be God. The Church has had a long tradition of warning Christians about "the world, the flesh, and the Devil." These are the temptations that Jesus fought in the desert (Mt 4:1–11). Satan urged Jesus to throw himself off the top of the Temple to prove his power (the pride of the world), to turn the stones to bread (comforting the flesh), and to bow down and worship him (the Devil).

The temptations that we face in ministry are not as dramatic, but they are no less lethal. The voice of the world would have us seek our own glory and avoid anything that might embarrass us. Pope Francis wrote, "It is striking that even some who clearly have solid doctrinal and spiritual convictions frequently fall into a lifestyle which leads to an attachment to financial security, or to a desire for power or human glory at all cost, rather than giving their lives to others in mission" (*Evangelii Gaudium*, 80).

The voice of the flesh desires our comfort. When ministry gets hard, we seek an easier way out. Pope Benedict XVI, at the beginning of his pontificate, reminded us, "Christ did not promise an easy life. Those who desire comforts have dialed the wrong number. Rather, he shows us the way to great things, the good, towards an authentic human life."

And the Devil? Yes, there is a devil. Saint Paul wrote, "Draw your strength from the Lord and from his mighty power. … to stand firm against the tactics of the devil. For our struggle is not with flesh and blood but with the principalities, with the powers, with the world rulers of this present darkness, with the evil spirits in the heavens" (Eph 6:10–12). Pray for help from your guardian angel, pray the St. Michael the Archangel prayer, and don't forget to sincerely pray the most powerful prayer of all, the Our Father, which concludes, "deliver us from evil" (also translated as "deliver us from the evil one").

It is good to be aware of these voices, but it's not useful to give them too much focus. Our focus should be on God. "The truth will set you free" (Jn 8:32). I'm told that in the United States Secret Service, which is responsible for dealing with counterfeit money, part of the training is to spend a lot of time looking at legitimate US currency. Trainees crumple it in their hands to get the feel of the paper. They stare at it under a magnifying glass to remember every detail. They even hold it up to their nose to smell it! They don't focus their time studying all the ways that currency could be counterfeit. They focus on the real thing so that they can tell when something is off.

The same is true in our spiritual lives. Don't worry about the lies; focus on the Spirit of truth. Prayerfully read the Scriptures, which the Spirit inspired, especially the Gospels. Reflect on the doctrines of the Church, which the Spirit authenticates. Recognize the Spirit in "the sacramental liturgy, through its words and symbols, in which the Holy Spirit puts us into communion with Christ" (CCC 688). This is why spending consistent time in prayer, both personal and communal, is essential in ministry. When we get used to the voice of the Spirit in the quiet of our prayer, we are quicker to recognize that voice in the cacophony of our lives.

The Autobiography Trap

One of the greatest traps in youth ministry is that we minister to the teen we *were*, not the teens they *are*. We can evaluate every new idea by unconsciously asking ourselves, "Would I have liked that when I was a teen?" We can pick topics based on what we heard, or wish we had heard, when we were in junior high or high school. We can presume that, because we were twelve or fifteen once, we know exactly what this teenager needs.

Though you were once a teenager, and there are certainly

some points of commonality, the youths we serve are different people living in a dramatically different culture. Be careful of this "autobiography" trap; it is a common one! It is better to approach young people more eager to learn about who they are than to teach about what you think that they should know.

The autobiography trap can happen to us both individually and collectively. I've seen entire youth retreats or programs that feel stuck in the early 2000s. "If it ain't broke, don't fix it," they say. "Not broken" doesn't mean that it is effective. There is a difference between a program going smoothly and the participants becoming saints. Though the Gospel message never changes, those to whom the Gospel is proclaimed "are profoundly linked to a culture, and the building up of the kingdom cannot avoid borrowing the elements of human culture or cultures" (*Evangelii Nuntiandi*, 20). What we say and do should reflect the lives, passions, and culture of the young people to whom we minister.

If I'm honest, I'd prefer simple math over Spirit-led ministry. One plus one always equals two, three times three always equals nine, and playing "Oceans" (or insert the latest emotional worship song here) during adoration will always make teenage girls cry. I like being in control. Don't we all? There were certainly times in ministry when I tried to replicate what the Spirit had done earlier, but without calling on the Holy Spirit to help in the current situation. I deserved the same rebuke that Saint Paul had for the Church in Galatia: "Are you so stupid? After beginning with the Spirit, are you now ending with the flesh?" (Gal 3:3).

This mistake was largely due to me thinking that it was "my" ministry, as if I was in control. Pope St. John Paul II wrote that those who are called to be missionaries (and I would include those who minister with youths in that category) must have a spirituality that "is expressed first of all by a life of complete docility to the Spirit" (*Redemptoris Missio*, 87). To be docile is to be "easy to teach." The opposite of docility is stubbornness, being unteachable (always thinking that you are the expert), and hard-heartedness. "Therefore, as the holy Spirit says: 'Oh, that today you would hear his voice, harden not your hearts'" (Heb 3:7–8).

Docility to the Spirit acknowledges that he is the teacher, and I am the student. He is the leader, and I am the follower. I don't ask the Holy Spirit to help me in *my* ministry. This is the Spirit's ministry; I surrender to *him*. The Holy Spirit has a lifelong plan for this person whom he loves. I'm just in it for a moment. It may be a part of his plan to use me in a powerful way in this teenager's life. If so, I want to be open to that. I keep in mind the words that God said to Zerubbabel, that he would succeed, "Not by might, and not by power, but by my spirit" (Zec 4:6). So, I keep praying, "*Come, Holy Spirit!*"

I DON'T ASK THE HOLY SPIRIT TO HELP ME IN MY MINISTRY. THIS IS THE SPIRIT'S MINISTRY; I SURRENDER TO HIM.

Different Ways of Hearing God's Voice

Another thing that helps me avoid the autobiography trap is considering the different ways that people hear the voice of God. I drew this understanding from a wonderful book by Fr. Benedict Groeschel, CFR, called *Spiritual Passages: The Psychology of Spiritual Development*. He wrote: "Western philosophy suggests that human beings know and seek God as the One, the True, the Good, and the Beautiful. If you analyze yourself and those you know well in terms of the spiritual life, you will notice that most people fit rather well into one or perhaps two categories." God — who is One, True, Good, and Beautiful — speaks in one voice. However, people are attuned to different ways of hearing that voice and respond to it in different ways.

Those who respond to God as *One* are either all in or all

out. They desire total intellectual and emotional integration in their life. Father Groeschel suggests St. Catherine of Genoa as an example of this. Those who respond to God as *True* love to study and ask questions. St. Thomas Aquinas is a wonderful example of one who experienced God as *Truth*. St. Francis of Assisi responded to God as *Good*. Those who hear God this way have a sensitive heart that desires to love and serve others, especially those most in need. Those who encounter God as *Beauty* will often say that their most powerful moment of experiencing God happened staring at a starry night or at a sunset on a beautiful beach. Saint Augustine famously wrote in his *Confessions*, "Late have I loved thee, O Beauty so ancient and so new," and in that same book asks, "How can we love anything but the beautiful?"

One way is not better than another, though Groeschel cautions that each of these ways can have a downside if not balanced by the others. The *One* may dramatically turn away from the Faith in the same way that he or she once accepted it, or harshly judge the contradictions that they see in themselves or others. The *True* can get distracted in academic study and consider the Faith as a subject to be studied instead of a person to be loved. The *Good* can become easily discouraged by the overwhelming suffering and evils in the world, often wondering why a good God would let bad things happen. The *Beautiful* can be "a complicated group" because beauty and pleasure are "two-sides of the same experience." They can settle for natural beauty instead of reaching for the supernatural.

Of these descriptions, which one (or two) do you think best describes you? Which one do you hear the loudest? Which one do you hear most quietly? A loose parallel could be drawn with the command to "love the Lord your God with all your heart, with all your soul, with all your mind, and with all your strength" (Mk 12:30). We can find it easier to experience God's love (and show our love for God) through our mind (*True*), our heart

(*Good*), our soul (*Beautiful*), and our strength (*One*). However, our inclination toward one does not excuse inactivity in another. If God as *True* is at the bottom of your list, you still need to take time to know the truths of the Faith, even though it will be tougher for you to hear his voice in that.

I'm not proposing this as a new kind of Myers-Briggs test for our spiritual lives! This is less of a definition of who we are and more a description of how we, and others, might hear God the best.

A Personal Reflection

For me, I experience God most profoundly as *Beautiful*. Put me in a beautiful Church with inspiring music, and I feel like I'm in heaven! The next loudest way I hear God is *True* (I love to study), then *One*, and the quietest would be *Good*. Unfortunately, when I started doing ministry, I didn't understand these distinctions in myself or in others. I thought that God spoke the same way to all people, and therefore the way I heard him must be the same way as everyone else. My early attempts at ministry were all about the *Beautiful*. The room where we held our youth nights looked like a theatrical production. The flyers were full color. Only the best musicians for the worship time!

There was nothing wrong with that. Many of the teens loved it (especially the theater kids). But I didn't give balanced attention to the other frequencies of God's voice. One teen asked if we might have a small group that studied early Church Fathers. I nodded as if I thought it was a good idea, but in my head I thought, "NERD ALERT!" I didn't realize that he most deeply encountered God as *True*. What he was really asking was, "Can you help me experience God in a way that I hear him best?" I'm glad that I wasn't foolish enough to say what I thought out loud, but I regret not being wise enough to listen.

It took me took too long to let teens experience God as *Good* by offering service opportunities. Since I wasn't as excited about them as I was about other aspects of ministry, they unconsciously fell on the back burner until some of my volunteers called me on that (thank God for candor!). When I saw how well the teens responded, it was a "Huh?" moment for me. Later, when I read Father Groeschel's book, it all made sense.

Father Groeschel doesn't assign any blame for how people hear God best, and neither should we. (Though it is honestly a bit embarrassing to admit that I don't "hear" God as well when serving others — and I'm a deacon!) On a personal level, it is a challenge to get outside of our comfort zone. From a ministry perspective, it is a reminder that people hear the voice of God in different ways, and that we don't want to limit them to how *we* hear him best.

There are also distinctions within these categories as well. For example, even if I encounter a teen who hears God best as *Beautiful*, he or she might have a different understanding of what "beauty" is. Pope Francis wrote, "We must be bold enough to discover new signs and new symbols … including those unconventional modes of beauty which may mean little to the evangelizers, yet prove particularly attractive for others" (*Evangelii Gaudium*, 167).

That last line applies to all of the above. Things about God that might mean less to you or me can be immensely attractive to others (and vice versa). We need to ask the Spirit to open our ears so that we can hear and proclaim him in new ways, not just the ways we prefer.

Guided by the Spirit

I won't pretend to be a connoisseur of video workout programs, but in the few that I have seen, the workout leaders all remind the viewer to *breathe*. Breathing is sometimes defined as a "semi-unconscious reflex," meaning that we can do it automatically or manually, depending on the situation (unlike our heartbeat, which is an automatic reflex). Taking a deep breath and holding it in gives us a rush of oxygen and tightens our core, giving us a momentary burst of energy and strength. But it is only a temporary high that can lead to negative consequences (like becoming unconscious) if we stop breathing.

I'd say that the Holy Spirit is also a kind of "semi-unconscious reflex," given to us at baptism. He is always at work in us, for "in him we live and move and have our being" (Acts 17:28). Yet we also can choose when to let him be more active in our lives (breathe deeper) or to "hold our breath" and shut him out. Sadly, just as we might stop breathing when doing heavy physical work, we can stop breathing in the Holy Spirit when things get tough in ministry by freaking out and trying to control everything ourselves. We start in the Spirit, move to the flesh, and end up unconscious.

This is also known as *burnout.* When Moses first saw God in a burning bush, he was surprised that "although the bush was on fire, it was not being consumed" (Ex 3:2). Yes, the Holy Spirit sets us on fire, but he never burns us out. Pope Francis wrote, "Yet there is no greater freedom than that of allowing oneself to be guided by the Holy Spirit, renouncing the attempt to plan and control everything to the last detail, and instead letting him enlighten, guide and direct us, leading us wherever he wills. The Holy Spirit knows well what is needed in every time and place. This is what it means to be mysteriously fruitful!" (*Evangelii Gaudium*, 280).

PLANS ARE NECESSARY, BUT THEY MUST BE INSPIRED BY THE HOLY SPIRIT IF THEY ARE TO BEAR ANY REAL FRUIT.

Jesus was one with the Spirit, so he knew where to go and what to say in his ministry with the woman at the well. We, as "little Christs," need to remind ourselves that this is the Spirit's ministry, not our own, and to consciously breathe in the Holy Spirit when we are tempted to take control. St. John Paul II wrote, "There is a temptation which perennially besets every spiritual journey and pastoral work: that of thinking that the results depend on our ability to act and to plan" (*Novo Millennio Ineunte*, 38). Plans are necessary, but they must be inspired by the Holy Spirit if they are to bear any real fruit. "Techniques of evangelization are good, but even the most advanced ones could not replace the gentle action of the Spirit" (*Evangelii Nuntiandi*, 75). We must quiet ourselves to listen to the Spirit, recognizing his voice over ours and the other voices that would distract us. Most importantly, we must trust that we will be given the right things to say and do at the right time, "For the holy Spirit will teach you at that moment what you should say" (Lk 12:12). God's timing is perfect. Though it can make us nervous that he doesn't show up early, we can be confident that he never shows up late.

Don't try to share God's Word without God's breath. *Come, Holy Spirit!*

Questions for Reflection and Discussion

- What did you learn (or were you reminded) about the Holy Spirit?
- How have you fallen into the "autobiography trap" in your ministry with teens, and what can you do in the future to avoid that?
- Using Father Groeschel's categories, which way do you hear God most clearly? Which way is the hardest for you to hear?
- How can you become more docile to the Holy Spirit, especially in your accompaniment with teenagers? Try to come up with some practical ideas.

10
Putting First Things First

This parable of Jesus always cuts me to the heart:

> Who among you would say to your servant who has just come in from plowing or tending sheep in the field, "Come here immediately and take your place at table"? Would he not rather say to him, "Prepare something for me to eat. Put on your apron and wait on me while I eat and drink. You may eat and drink when I am finished"? Is he grateful to that servant because he did what was commanded? So should it be with you. When you have done all you have been commanded, say, "We are unprofitable servants; we have done what we were obliged to do." (Luke 17:7–10)

Though I was familiar with this parable and probably heard it many times in my life, it was in my fourth year of ministry that it really hit me. *I* was the servant who worked in the field all day but wouldn't serve the Master at night. I had fallen into the most common trap of youth ministry, or any ministry for that matter: I had substituted my relationship with Jesus for my ministry with others.

I had been trying to live by spiritual osmosis, thinking that if I was around enough holy events it would eventually rub off on me. At a holy hour for teens, I'd be far more focused on the kids in the back than the Eucharist on the altar. At Mass, I paid more attention to the songs that I led than the Scripture that was proclaimed. The homily became a great time to sneak out and check the youth room to make sure that things were ready for the following meeting. My prayer time became my prep time. Any spiritual insight that I had was immediately applied to a youth group talk.

And I was tired. *So tired.* It felt like I was at the end of a long run, barely able to put one foot in front of the other, pushing myself to the point of collapse. Yet I told myself that I had to keep going. For the teens. For the volunteers. For the parish.

You might notice that "Jesus" wasn't in that list. Honestly, I was kind of mad at Jesus. Ministry wasn't going as well as it had gone before. What more did he want me to do? I couldn't possibly work harder. I felt the same kind of anger that Martha had when she asked Jesus, "Lord, do you not care?" (Lk 10:40).

I was in that mindset when I read that parable. My first thought was, "Great, more work! After working all day I'm supposed to make you supper, too?" But then I read it more closely. After we provide him food and drink, he provides *us* food and drink. And what is the food and drink that Jesus provides us? His very Body and Blood. It reminded me of the passage from the *Catechism* about prayer: "Prayer is the encounter of God's thirst with ours. God thirsts that we may thirst for him" (2560). God hungers, he thirsts, for us. When we give him ourselves in return, he satisfies our every longing.

I had been going to bed each night without my spiritual supper. I had been spending so much time in the field that I had left no time for the Master. I was serving the household of the Lord, not the Lord of the household.

Mixed Motivations

I have a hard time with unconditional love. Sure, I talk about it all the time. I get the concept. But it is really hard to accept. Though I knew "what" God wanted me to do (ministry with young people), I hadn't really understood "why." My assumption was that my life in ministry was to "pay him back" for all that he had done for me, and to earn some of the grace that I had been given by helping others.

I WAS SERVING THE HOUSEHOLD OF THE LORD, NOT THE LORD OF THE HOUSEHOLD.

Here's the thing. God never asks us to pay anything back. He invites us to pay things forward.

There is a huge difference between giving because you owe and sharing because you love. The first makes you a prisoner, crippled forever by an insurmountable debt. It leads to grumbling, complaining, and disillusionment. Saint Paul wrote, "You did not receive a spirit of slavery to fall back into fear, but you received a spirit of adoption, through which we cry, 'Abba, Father!'" (Rom 8:15). We are not his slaves, and God is not our boss. He is our Father. We are his sons and daughters.

When I saw myself as "Bob Rice, Youth Minister" before God, it was all about the ministry. When it went well, I felt that he loved me; when it struggled, I thought that I was being punished. I replaced "who I am" with "what I do." Yes, I *do* ministry with young people, but I *am* a child of God. That never changes. That can never be "bought" or paid back. "For by grace you have been saved through faith, and this is not from you; it is the gift of God; it is not from works, so no one may boast" (Eph 2:8–9).

I have trypanophobia (which is a cooler way of saying that

I'm scared of needles), so I would never get a tattoo. But if I wasn't afraid of needles, I would tattoo that verse backward on my chest. That way, I could read it every morning when I look in the mirror and be reminded that my adoption is a gift from God that does not need to be earned, just accepted — and shared.

"Payback" is my personal struggle in ministry. What is yours? I've worked with people who do ministry because of *fear*. "If I don't do this, God will send me to hell!" or "He won't do things for me if I don't do things for him." Then there are *fixers*. "These kids need someone to straighten them out — if their parents won't do it, I will!" Then there is *pride*, the root of all sins. Yes, I've struggled with that one, too. We like being seen as saints and find ways to ever-so-subtly (or not so subtly) mention in conversations how tired we are because we were just on a weekend ministering to teenagers (and then pause for their compliments).

I remember confessing to a priest one time that my motives in ministry were not 100 percent pure. He burst out laughing! "Me neither," he said with a smile. "When you figure out how to do that, let me know!"

You're just going to have to get comfortable with your mixed motivations for doing ministry. Since you can't manage what you don't mention, acknowledge some of the "wrong" reasons before God and ask for his grace to focus on the "right" reason, which is God himself.

Another way of saying this is don't let the "fruits" become the "root." The fruits of ministry can (at times) be popular acclaim, a feeling of self-satisfaction, joy at seeing a kid change his or her life in the right direction, a confidence that God is with you and that you are doing the right thing, and so forth. In rare moments, it might even make you money! It's OK to enjoy the fruits when they come, but don't focus on them. Instead, be focused on the roots: our love for Jesus. That love of Jesus overflows into our love of teenagers.

Boundaries

God is more concerned with the ministry that he does *for* you than the ministry that he does *with* you. You are not a means to an end. Though there are many sacrifices involved in ministry with youths, you are *never* asked to sacrifice your relationship with Jesus or things necessary for your physical or mental health. Jesus died for the teens you serve; you don't have to. One death was enough!

GOD IS MORE CONCERNED WITH THE MINISTRY THAT HE DOES FOR YOU THAN THE MINISTRY THAT HE DOES WITH YOU.

It is essential to have boundaries, both in ministry and in life. *You* have to know how much you can give and when to say no. Nobody can figure that out for you. The harvest is so abundant and there are so many needs in ministry, it is easy to give and give and give until you have nothing left.

There are unhealthy people everywhere; Catholic ministry is no exception. Some priests, campus ministers, parish youth ministers, or "all of the above" are workaholics, addicted to the pace. These aren't great people to do ministry with. When people don't have good boundaries for themselves, they usually don't have them for others.

Boundaries are especially important if you are married. Nothing breaks my heart more than to see marriages break up or families suffer because the husband or wife spent more time with ministry than their family. Let me make this clear: *This is not of God.* Your first vocation is your relationship with Jesus, the call to holiness. If you are married, your second vocation is to your spouse and any children you may have. For a time, you may have a calling to minister with young people or others, but it should never interfere with those first two vocations. God would never ask you to prioritize time with teenagers over your spouse and children.

Ministry with youths requires many sacrifices of time and energy. Yes, there were times I missed things in my children's lives to respond to ministry needs with teenagers. I always navigated those things with my spouse. Should I help with this retreat, though it might mean missing one of my kid's soccer games? We prayed about it. If I could make all the other soccer games that season and we thought the Lord wanted me on the retreat, we said yes. Otherwise, we said no. It worked the other way, too: If something came up in my spouse's or my children's lives where they needed me, I got someone else to take care of the ministry.

As an ordained deacon, I gave a sacred vow of obedience to my bishop. But the bishop only ordained me because my wife gave him permission to do so. My brother deacons and I refer to our spouses as our "first bishops." If she says no, we don't go. That is a good model for all married ministers, lay or ordained.

Those of you who are single may have more time to devote to ministry, but that shouldn't mean *all* your time. If you sacrifice all your leisure time and other social relationships, you might just stay single forever (even if you are called to marriage). It is important to have friends who are outside of ministry, pursue hobbies, go on dates, and the like.

Jesus said, "Let your 'Yes' mean 'Yes,' and your 'No' mean 'No'" (Mt 5:37). Having the freedom to say no will make your yes more meaningful. "Catholic guilt" is not a healthy motivation, "for God loves a cheerful giver" (2 Cor 9:7). Saying no to a ministry opportunity is not always the same as saying no the Lord. The harvest is so abundant that you can't do everything. Recall the previous warning: The Devil will push you do more than God asks.

Finding Balance

Though ministry cannot not be a substitution for our spirituality, God will use it as an opportunity to help us grow in holiness. When I began training for a 10K run, I started on my treadmill. The nice thing about treadmills is that you can hit "stop" when you get tired, and I did so frequently! When I started to run outside, I immediately noticed two things. First there were *hills*. That made it harder to run. Second, there was no "stop" button. If you ran a mile away, you had to run a mile back. It got tougher, but it also got more rewarding. I grew stronger and was able to run faster and farther.

Getting into ministry is like moving from the treadmill to the track. It pushes you more. It takes you outside your comfort zone. It can be scary at times, too. But that is where the miracles happen. You get to see God do things that you would never see sitting in the pew or your prayer chair at home.

I wish that more Catholics understood this. I worry that some spend all their time in a "spiritual gym" but never compete in the race or "fight the good fight." They're doing the very thing that Saint Paul cautioned us to avoid: "Thus I do not run aimlessly; I do not fight as if I were shadowboxing" (1 Cor 9:26). We don't pray to be more effective in ministry. We pray to more deeply experience and be transformed by the merciful love of God. But remember what I quoted previously from St. Paul VI: "It is unthinkable that a person should accept the Word and give himself to the kingdom without becoming a person who bears witness to it and proclaims it in his turn" (*Evangelii Nuntiandi*, 24). The visible fruit of how we give our hearts to Jesus is how we share our lives with others. "So also faith of itself, if it does not have works, is dead" (Jas 2:17).

Everyone who is baptized is called to some kind of ministry. I've had people say that their "ministry" is their family and friends, and they don't have time for anyone else. Everyone's life is different, and one might have more demanding needs in their family or among their friends than others. However, keep in mind the words of Jesus: "For if you love those who love you, what credit is that to you? Even sinners love those who love them. And if you do good to those who do good to you, what credit is that to you? Even sinners do the same" (Lk 6:32–33). We are not only called to share the love of God with those who love us, but also called to share that love with those we don't yet know.

IF GOD IS CALLING YOU TO IT, HE WILL GIVE YOU TIME TO DO IT. HE CREATED "TIME," AFTER ALL.

It is all about finding balance. Balance begins with putting first things first. Our relationship with Jesus, expressed in prayer (personal prayer, Mass, sacraments, etc.) is foundational. Next are our other sacramental responsibilities or sacred commitments, such as family, priesthood, marriage, diaconate, and/or religious or consecrated life. There are also our basic needs, such as physical health (staying in shape, getting sleep, eating healthy), emotional well-being (social life, healthy leisure, the counsel of good friends or, if necessary, professionals), and financial needs (work, having a balanced budget, etc.).

With that list, you might wonder if there is time for anything else! If God is calling you to it, he will give you time to do it. He created "time," after all. Be neither stingy nor wasteful with the time that God has given you. Be kind to yourself as you seek to find balance. Sometimes you will overcommit and have to tough it out; other times you will say no to something when you could have said yes, and you only realize that later. Opportunities are plentiful, and nobody is perfect. Above all, "Seek first the kingdom [of God] and his righteousness, and all these things will be given you besides" (Mt 6:33).

Questions for Reflection and Discussion

- What titles or perception of yourself do you have that get in the way of seeing yourself primarily as a son or daughter of God?
- Since you can't manage what you don't mention, what are some of the "unhealthy" attitudes that you may struggle with when doing ministry with youths?
- How do you (or could you) help those in authority "fulfill their task with joy and not with sorrow"?
- How is your balance between prayer, life, and ministry? Are you making enough time for God (daily personal prayer time,* Mass, sacraments, etc.)?

* Sometimes people ask how much time they should spend a day in personal prayer. St. Francis de Sales, writing for laypeople (those who worked in business or at home), suggested, "Set aside an hour every day before the mid-day meal, if possible early in the morning, when your mind is less distracted and fresher after the night's rest. Don't extend it for more than an hour unless your spiritual director expressly tells you to do so" (Francis de Sales, *Introduction to the Devout Life*, pt. 2, chap. 1, no. 3). If you think that they were less busy back then, I propose that you underestimate humanity's inherent ability to waste time (even before the internet was created). If an hour seems daunting, start small and try to slowly increase your time by trying different ways of prayer: a Rosary, spiritual reading, Liturgy of the Hours, etc.

11
The Letter of Our Hearts

It is easy to imagine Moses standing on the mountain before the recently emancipated Hebrews, holding two stone tablets containing the commandments of God, especially if you have seen *The Ten Commandments* or *The Prince of Egypt* (or Mel Brooks's *History of the World: Part I*). The commandments were more than a list of dos and don'ts. The Hebrews had been Egyptian slaves for hundreds of years. They only knew Egyptian ways. The struggles that the Hebrews had over the next few decades (and even centuries) with being obedient to God could be summed up as, "You can take the Hebrew out of Egypt, but you can't take Egypt out of the Hebrew." It was as if God's commands were something external to them, something foreign.

So, God spoke to the prophet Jeremiah, "See, days are coming … when I will make a new covenant with the house of Israel and the house of Judah. It will not be like the covenant I made with their ancestors the day I took them by the hand to lead them out of the land of Egypt. … I will place my law within them, and write it upon their hearts; I will be their God, and they shall be my people" (Jer 31:31–33). This is the covenant of Jesus Christ! In our baptism, "the love of God has been poured out into our hearts through the holy Spirit that has been given to us" (Rom 5:5).

Saint Paul told those who were believers that *they* were now "a letter of Christ ... written not in ink but by the Spirit of the living God, not on tablets of stone but on tablets that are hearts of flesh" (2 Cor 3:3). One no longer needs to look to tablets of stone to see how God wants us to live. His law of love is written in hearts of flesh, the hearts of those who believe in Jesus and follow his ways.

Wait a second. That's us, right? So, if people want to know what it means to be a disciple of Jesus Christ ... they have to read our hearts?

Becoming a "Teenager"

Saint Paul wrote many challenging things to those in ministry, and this (I think) is one of the most difficult ones:

> Although I am free in regard to all, I have made myself a slave to all so as to win over as many as possible. To the Jews I became like a Jew to win over Jews; to those under the law I became like one under the law — though I myself am not under the law — to win over those under the law. To those outside the law I became like one outside the law — though I am not outside God's law but within the law of Christ — to win over those outside the law. To the weak I became weak, to win over the weak. I have become all things to all, to save at least some. All this I do for the sake of the gospel, so that I too may have a share in it. (1 Corinthians 9:19–23)

So, to the teenager do we become ... *a teenager*? For some, going back to seventeen doesn't seem so bad. But *middle school*? I don't know of anyone who wants to redo being twelve.

Thankfully, Saint Paul isn't suggesting we be something we are not. When we read his letters and about his life (in the Acts of the Apostles), he doesn't come across as a con artist or chameleon. He does, however, find creative ways to connect to the cultures of those with whom he is doing ministry. In Thessalonica, he made tents and integrated himself into the working community. In Athens, he quoted Greek poetry and incorporated their religious imagery to explain the Gospel. He spent time with all the communities in which he did ministry — not just months, but years.

Gentiles could tell by looking at him that Paul was a Jew. Yet Paul didn't treat them like Jews normally did. To their surprise, he even seemed knowledgeable about their philosophies, faiths, and cultures. Most importantly, Paul didn't close himself off in a synagogue or only spend time with prominent Jewish leaders. He was available, approachable, and even preached his message in public places where everyone could listen. Paul was certainly a Jew — but he spoke and lived in such a manner that those in Gentile communities would say, "He is one of us."

In a similar way, we have to become a "teen" to the teenager. We need not wear popular fashion or use current slang (please, I beg you, *don't*). Instead, we need to understand their cultures: the family that they are from, the high school that they attend, the music that they listen to, the shows that they watch, and the like. We need to be present and available to them, measuring time not in months but years. And we need to treat each one of them not just as a random teenager to whom we aren't related, but as a younger brother or sister in Christ. My hope is that, when a teen thinks of me, he or she doesn't think I am "one of *them*" but more like "one of *us*."

When we share the Gospel with them, we should do it as

Jesus did. Jesus explained some of the greatest mysteries of God using simple things around him: fig trees, flowers, sheep, kings and servants, fathers and sons. We need to create contemporary "cultural parables" for teenagers by learning about their cultures and finding things within their lives that point to God. Or, as the Second Vatican Council wrote, to "gladly and reverently lay bare the seeds of the Word which lie hidden among their fellows" (*Ad Gentes*, 11). Though truths of the Faith are clearly articulated in the *Catechism of the Catholic Church*, one cannot simply pass on the Faith by handing someone a book. The Gospel message must be *enculturated*, that is, proclaimed in a way that can be understood using the vocabulary and imagery that they are familiar with: "The kingdom which the Gospel proclaims is lived by men who are profoundly linked to a culture, and the building up of the kingdom cannot avoid borrowing the elements of human culture or cultures" (*Evangelii Nuntiandi*, 20). This is not "watering down" the teaching of the Faith, but instead it is creatively presenting the truths of the Faith in a way that can resonate with its listeners.

WE NEED TO CREATE CONTEMPORARY "CULTURAL PARABLES" FOR TEENAGERS BY LEARNING ABOUT THEIR CULTURES AND FINDING THINGS WITHIN THEIR LIVES THAT POINT TO GOD.

Jesus not only did this with his teaching but with his very life, the Incarnation. He became flesh and "made his dwelling among us" (Jn 1:14). The Greek word translated as "made his dwelling among" also means to "pitch one's tent." This is also the root of the word *tabernacle*. Just as Jesus "tabernacles" with his Church in the Eucharist, so we, a community of missionary disciples, must go forth and "pitch our tents" among those who do not know him, sharing the Gospel through sharing our lives.

Understanding Accompaniment

American culture has been structured to divide adults from adolescents. We lock them away in high schools and keep them busy with activities, abandoning them to form a culture unto themselves. Crossing that cultural divide is one of the most difficult things about ministry with teenagers. But it *has* to be done — THERE IS NO OTHER WAY. Christ can't be proclaimed by carrier pigeon. What teens currently see on their phones about Catholicism is not attractive, and much of it is even repulsive. No wonder so many of them are leaving the Faith!

Accompaniment is a nonnegotiable of youth ministry. Young people need to "see" what a disciple of Jesus looks like before they can become disciples themselves. That means that we need to "dwell" among them as Jesus did with us. We need to spend time with them. We need to listen to them. We need to care about what they care about. We need to go out of our way to help them, even suffer for them. Pope Francis wrote, "Young people need to be approached with the grammar of love, not by being preached at. The language that young people understand is spoken by those who radiate life, by those who are there for them and with them" (*Christus Vivit*, 211). We can only share Jesus who is "written in our hearts" by sharing our hearts with others.

Let me start with some erroneous stereotypes. Accompaniment is NOT:

- *Becoming "best friends" with teenagers.* We aren't their age and don't need to pretend that we are. We can't replace their need for good relationships with their peers, but we can provide them with good relationships with adults (us). Though we will do everything we can to be there when they need us, we have our own lives (work, family, etc.) and are not available 24/7.

- *Forced or manipulative.* A young person should never feel guilted, forced, or coerced into a relationship with an adult, and an adult should not "fake" anything to have a friendship with a teen. I heard of one youth minister who had a sign-up sheet for teens who might want to hang out with him. Nobody did — relationships don't work like that.
- *Isolating.* Pope Francis says that our ministry with the young should never "isolate young people from their family and the larger community, or turn them into a select few, protected from all contamination" (*Christus Vivit*, 30). Recall the earlier definition of youth ministry: It is about the community responding to the needs of teenagers so that they can share their gifts in return.
- *Pointless.* "What's the point of accompanying young people if they are walking away from the Church?" Just as Jesus was willing to walk in the wrong direction for a few miles to unpack the Scriptures to the disciples on the road to Emmaus, we need to join young people on their path before we can model for them a new way to go. We love them enough to meet them where they are, but we love them too much to leave them there.

Here are some things that accompaniment IS:

- *Natural and genuine.* You will make a connection with some teens. You won't with others. Honestly, it might be fair to say you won't with *most* of the teens. Though we offer relationships to everyone, only a few might take us up on it, and that is OK. These become the relationships that last long after the program is over. These are the life-changing relationships (for them and for you) that make ministry worth it.

- *Confident.* We believe that "there already exists in individuals and peoples an expectation, even if an unconscious one, of knowing the truth about God. … The missionary's enthusiasm in proclaiming Christ comes from the conviction that he is responding to that expectation" (*Redemptoris Missio*, 45). Jesus is alive in us and wants to love young people through us. We're not worried that we're forcing anything down their throat. This is the very thing that they were made for!
- *Communal.* We accompany as a *community*, and that begins with their families (see below). Young people need to see numerous examples of disciples of Jesus living out their faith in different ways.
- *Transparent.* If a young person is in need of frequent one-on-one psychological attention (and some are), that is what counselors are for. That's not us. Everything that we do is out in the open. We get to know their families and communicate who we are and what we are about. We keep each other accountable.
- *Patient.* It's not a quick fix. This ministry is less like surgery and more like ongoing physical therapy. We have to be "patient and compassionate with others, and to find the right way to gain their trust, their openness and their readiness to grow" (*Evangelii Gaudium*, 172).

The above isn't meant to be an exhaustive list, nor is "relational ministry" an exact science. It varies depending on the people involved, the cultures that they are from, and the environment that they are in. President Theodore Roosevelt famously said, "No one cares how much you know until they know how much you care." Accompaniment is taking the time to get to know teenagers, opening our hearts to them, and showing them that we care.

Places of Accompaniment

Where do we start? Are we supposed to walk up to a group of teens in a mall and ask, "Will you be my friends?" Uh, *no*. It begins by creating places of accompaniment within our current programs of ministry with youths, and then expanding those opportunities by connecting with the teens we know at various school or community events, meeting their friends as we do.

I can't speak to every ministry context with teenagers, but here are some examples. A youth group meets for an hour and a half every Sunday evening. It starts at 7:00 p.m. and is packed with content and activities until 8:30 p.m. (sometimes running longer, much to the parents' dismay). If the goal was to get as much information to the teens as possible, *mission accomplished*.

But what if the goal also included creating spaces where adults and teens could get to know each other? Perhaps you'd have activities within that time that teens and adults could do together. Maybe end the "program" at eight-ish and have time for some good homemade snacks (there is always someone in the parish ready to unleash their culinary talents on hungry and appreciative teenagers). Don't put the food out on a table; instead, have adults serve the teens. It is really easy to start a conversation with teens when you've got a plate of homemade cupcakes in your hand.

When you schedule social events, always ask the question, "How is this helping our adults and teens get to know each other?" If you go bowling, have adults spread out in the teams with youths (though adults vs. teens is good every once in a while, too!). If playing sports, do the same thing. St. John Bosco (the patron saint of youth ministry) never let his fellow priests be referees in games. They always had to be on teams with the boys. Adults and youths should be playing together, talking together, and having fun together. Relationships are built on shared experiences. Since those are few and far between in our culture, we have to create them in order to facilitate healthy adult and teen interaction.

If you are planning a weekend retreat, don't pack the afternoon with workshops that teens won't have the energy to listen to. Have structured free time activities with adults at every location: a volleyball tournament with Tim and Jack, a hike with Sarah and Mike, board games in the meeting room with Bill and Suzy. Don't forget that travel to and from the event is also a great time to talk and get to know teenagers.

We also need to go where the teens are: their high school. Get with at least one other person (going two by two isn't just a safe environment policy, it is biblical!) and cheer on those teenagers who are active in the ministry by going to their games, concerts, or plays. Pro tip: go to a game with fewer people, maybe even an away game. You'll not only be "seen" better, you will get to know the other families in the stands who are there for their kids. Wave goodbye at the end and say, "Great job!" You don't need a deep conversation; they just need to see you going the "second mile." I know some in youth ministry who volunteer to be an assistant coach for a team, run the stage crew for the play, or help with the cheerleaders. These are exceptional ways to be at their "well."

It is more challenging to do this if your parish has teens from multiple high schools. There is a strange logic that suggests that if you can't go to everyone then you shouldn't go to anyone.

That is foolishness. Go to what you can based on the teens who are involved in the ministry. Jesus spent most of his time with twelve guys, and even more of his time with three of them. It isn't playing favorites; it is doing as much as you can with the limited time and resources that you have. The harvest is abundant, but the laborers are few. There are always more needs than you can respond to, so do *something*.

Some adults argue that the best youth ministry is peer ministry, and that we should empower teens to minister among themselves. I agree that teens ministering to teens is important, as long as they are doing it side by side with loving adults. Teens ministering to teens with adults standing in the background doesn't represent what a community of faith should be (that looks more like a juvenile detention center!). To use nerdy language, ministry with young people should be both intragenerational and intergenerational.

MINISTRY WITH YOUNG PEOPLE SHOULD BE BOTH INTRAGENERATIONAL AND INTERGENERATIONAL.

Like Jesus at the well, a lot of relational ministry is simply making yourself available and *waiting*. Have you noticed how many miracles happened in the Gospels while Jesus was on the way to somewhere else? It wasn't just, "Meet me at the Mount on Sunday and you'll hear a great sermon." Don't get me wrong, that was a *great* sermon! Teaching moments like those are essential for any good ministry. But the majority of the famous stories of conversion and healing in the Bible — the paralytic lowered from the roof, blind Bartimaeus shouting from the side of the road, the woman with a hemorrhage crawling through a crowd to touch Jesus' garment, Zacchaeus in the tree, even the good thief on the cross — were "unscheduled" ministry moments.

I have found that to be true in my ministry with teens. I've seen profound moments of conversion and healing happen in a church, but I have also experienced sacred moments in a parking lot after a meeting, on the bus ride back from a retreat, in the waiting room of a hospital, waiting in line for a roller coaster at Cedar Point, or at a reception after a funeral. Those were the moments of accompaniment. That's where they got to see the "real" me, warts and all, and read the letter of Christ written on my fickle but faithful heart. Those were the moments when the power of Christ changed lives.

Don't let your evangelistic imagination be limited by my examples! I only provide them as a starting point for different ways that we might build relationships with teens so as to share the Faith through sharing our lives.

Obedience

If God calls us to ministry with youths, it is through the authority that he has given to his Bride, the Church. In a diocese, that authority is the bishop; in a parish, it is the pastor; in a religious order, it is the superior. We must realize that the ministry isn't ours, and the authority through which we minister is not our own. Many of our Protestant brothers and sisters believe that the Bible gives them the authority to preach where they want and do what they feel called to do. As Catholics, we have a hierarchical approach, believing that the missionary mandate to "Go … and make disciples" (Mt 28:19) was specifically given to the apostles first and from them comes down to us. Some dioceses don't even like calling lay people youth "ministers" (they use titles like "Coordinator of Youth Ministry") because they don't want to confuse ordained ministry with lay ministry. Though I don't personally have a problem with the term *youth minister*, I understand the tension.

I'm usually great about being obedient to those in charge …

until I disagree with them. I have had numerous ministry situations in which I disagreed with the direction and decisions of those in authority. My prideful heart was tempted to rebel (and when I did, it didn't go so well). After all, I'm the expert here! I know more than he does!

Those are the moments when, even if we're right, we're wrong. In the conclusion to the Letter to the Hebrews, it says, "Obey your leaders and defer to them, for they keep watch over you and will have to give an account, that they may fulfill their task with joy and not with sorrow, for that would be of no advantage to you" (Heb 13:17). Telling a pastor how to run his parish is akin to telling parents how to raise their kids. Sure, there are some obvious nonnegotiables. There is also room for different styles and approaches. My pastor was ordained by the Church and assigned by the bishop to run the parish. The ministry I and the volunteers do with the youths of the parish is an extension of *his* ministry, and I try to help him do it "with joy and not with sorrow." The Lord knows how much pressure many of our clergy are under!

The most difficult moments are when those in authority don't seem to care about young people, or at least not as much as we do. We might have the luxury of being singularly focused on youths, but they often have to balance the many needs of others with few resources. Stay positive and keep advocating for young people. Most importantly, *don't let someone else's lack of enthusiasm for ministering with teenagers diminish yours.*

Nobody gets a blank check in ministry. Remember, "God opposes the proud but bestows favor on the humble" (1 Pt 5:5). We all answer to somebody. If you can't work with that somebody, it would be better to leave than to run an underground resistance. There is enough division in the Church already, and there are plenty of opportunities to do ministry elsewhere. Saint Paul cautioned, "Whoever resists authority opposes what God has appointed, and those who oppose it will bring judgment upon themselves" (Rom 13:2).

Pray for those in authority in the Church. Pray for bishops, pastors, priests, and religious. Pray for lay leaders who are in charge of ministries and apostolates. The Devil would have us be quick to critique and accuse. In contrast, "Do everything without grumbling or questioning, that you may be blameless and innocent" (Phil 2:14–15). You will find blessing in obedience. Submitting when we disagree is an opportunity to grow in holiness.

Safe Relationships, Safe Environments

I remember watching my television on the morning of September 11, 2001. Watching the planes fly into the World Trade Center seemed like something out of a disaster movie. It was hard for my brain to process what I was seeing: America being attacked by terrorists. Such a thing was unimaginable up until that point. But there it was, right in front of me on my television.

I had a similar experience just a few months later in January of 2002. The Boston Globe began to run a series of articles about widespread sexual abuse of clergy and how it was being covered up by many bishops. Again, this was something unimaginable. But there it was, right in front of me on my computer screen.

Having been in ministry in the "before and after" of those scandals, I can say that we weren't doing a great job with relational ministry with teens *before*, but such ministry almost became nonexistent *after*. I find it unfortunate, and arguably unfair, that ministry with teenagers took the brunt of much of the restrictions and regulations that followed as the Church sought to establish clear policies and rebuild trust with the public. I'm not so naive as to suggest that there has not been scandal with lay people in ministry with teenagers, nor would I suggest that policies that protect teens and children aren't necessary today —

they certainly are. But it is also the case that more conversations need to occur as to what the best policies are, because as we focused on protecting teenagers from potential sexual abuse (and the Church from potential lawsuits) we also "protected" them from what they needed to become disciples of Jesus: healthy, mentoring relationships with loving adults in their faith community. In 2012, Frank Mercandante wrote in his book *Engaging a New Generation*: "Church leaders, as good stewards, do need to guard against further financial losses that would negatively impact many forms of ministry." But, he contined, "overly stringent policies lead to a Church that is more concerned about financial and legal protection than on the active, personal, pastoral care of young people. This results in the loss of the Church's credibility and the far greater loss of our teens."

Those words are still valid in many places in the United States today. Relational ministry and safe environments are not at odds with each other. They need each other. Teens can only enter into healthy relationships with adults if they feel that they are in an environment where they are protected and safe. This goes double for their families, who are rightly concerned about programs and people who may influence their child. Our actions and activities must not only be without a hint of impropriety, they should also be transparent, clearly communicated, and inviting to teens and their families.

In the two decades since the scandals became public, I've seen many dioceses adjusting their policies to hit the right balance of "protection" and "pastoral." Those have usually happened thanks to people in youth ministry asking questions, explaining the importance of relational ministry, and working out good compromises. As I emphasized in the previous section, this is not *our* ministry, and we need to be obedient to whatever policies are in place whether we consider them overly stringent or not. Remember, they are for our protection as well! Instead of having a reactive attitude ("I can't because they won't let me,") those in ministry with young people need to have a proactive approach to relational ministry ("What can I do within the current boundaries?"). You will find that you can create opportunities in the programs you offer teenagers to be more relational and discover new ways to connect with teens outside those programs in safe and healthy ways.

Thankfully, we are not called to do this on our own.

Part of an Evangelizing Community

Pope Francis wrote: "The community has an important role in the accompaniment of young people; it should feel collectively responsible for accepting, motivating, encouraging and challenging them. All should regard young people with understanding, appreciation and affection, and avoid constantly judging them or demanding of them a perfection beyond their years" (*Christus Vivit*, 243). This ministry cannot be done by a single individual, but requires an intragenerational, intergenerational, and intercultural community of disciples who are willing to do whatever it takes to reach the young:

> The Church which "goes forth" is a community of missionary disciples who. ... [get] involved by word and deed in people's daily lives; it bridges distances, it is willing to abase itself if necessary, and it embraces human life, touching the suffering flesh of Christ in others. Evangelizers thus take on the "smell of the sheep" and the sheep are willing to hear their voice (*Evangelii Gaudium*, 24).

Are we willing to draw so close to teenagers that we end up smelling like them? It sounds unpleasant, I know. Ministry can be hard and unpleasant. Teenage behavior frequently vacillates between awesome and annoying. It is easy to hang out with the "good" kids, the polite ones who were raised by their loving and faithful mom and dad, the ones who enjoy reading and going to church. I love those kids! But if that is the only group that we do ministry with, we essentially become the Good Catholic Teen Babysitting Club. We encourage isolation, not evangelization. We stay with the ninety-nine instead of searching for the one that is lost.

AS WE ACCOMPANY TEENAGERS, WE MUST ALSO ADVOCATE TO THE WIDER COMMUNITY TO BE AWARE OF THEIR NEEDS AND OPEN TO THEIR GIFTS.

When it comes to teenagers today, it feels more like the ratio is reversed: one sheep is safe and ninety-nine are lost. We have to go out, with emphasis on the word *we*. Lone rangers need not apply. We move slower as a group, but we also move stronger. Teenagers don't need a person; they need a people. You can be one of those people, but you are only one string in a net. Teenagers need to see people of different ages and different cultures living out their call to discipleship in different ways.

As we accompany teenagers, we must also advocate to the wider community to be aware of their needs and open to their gifts. Teenagers are too often "out of sight, out of mind" in our culture today, and often have no voice in our parishes or communities of faith. Adults often harbor (consciously or unconsciously) a generational bias toward adolescents. To quote George Orwell, "Every generation imagines itself to be more intelligent than the one that went before it, and wiser than the one that comes after it." This is nothing new. Even Saint Paul had to encourage Saint Timothy, "Let no one have contempt for your youth" (1 Tm 4:12).

You can probably guess the antidote to this generational

enmity: *relationships*. Creatively foster opportunities for older people to connect with, or at least to hear from young people. For example, after every retreat, I'd have a teenager share a brief testimony at the end of Mass. That gave an adult in the pew a new perspective of how much a young person cared about the Faith. I also worked with other ministries in the Church to see how they could be more welcoming to teenagers (and not just use them for physical labor). Ministry as a community can be challenging, but it is also the only way to be Church.

Partnering with Families

The first community we are a part of is our family. "Youth ministry can present the ideal of life in Christ as the process of building a house on rock. For most young people, that house, their life, will be built on marriage and married love," explained Pope Francis in *Christus Vivit*. "That is why youth ministry and the pastoral care of families should be coordinated and integrated, with the aim of ensuring a continuous and suitable accompaniment of the vocational process" (242).

In 2004, there was a groundbreaking study called the National Study of Youth and Religion (NSYR) where they interviewed both teenagers and their parents about their religious beliefs and practices. Contrary to the stereotype that teens often rebel against their family's faith, the survey found that teens are more likely than not to adopt the religious beliefs of their parents. In this survey, Catholic teens fared the worst when compared to their Protestant peers (contrary beliefs to the Church, lax religious attendance, etc.), and their parents fared just as badly. The author suggested, "Perhaps the issue is not U.S. Catholic *teen* religious practice at all, but overall U.S. Catholic religious practice generally, as engaged and modeled by adults."

The good news here is that if you have a ministry where a teenager willingly attends, it is likely because they have a supportive and faithful family who is encouraging them to go. Get to know those families! Make it clear that you want to partner with them in passing on the Faith to their teen. Drop them a note to thank them for their teen's involvement in the ministry and share a story about how he or she impressed you. In your programming, keep parents in the loop about everything that you are talking about, and make sure to have numerous open events where interested parents can attend. Seek their wisdom on how to more effectively engage their teen and their teenager's friends. Proactively cultivate positive relationships with the engaged families of teenagers in your parish. It will make a huge difference in your relationships with their teens and the ministry overall.

There is some bad news here, too. If you have a ministry that "requires" teenagers to be there (such as mandatory classes for confirmation preparation), chances are that many of the families are going to push against what you are requiring. You will even have families that will encourage behavior contrary to the Gospel. (I remember one parent telling me that I was crazy to tell their teen not to have sex before marriage!) These are difficult situations to navigate. As with ministry with youths, the key to good ministry with families is *relationships*. You are with their teen for a few short years; that teen is a part of their family forever (whether that teen likes it or not). Anything that you can do, no matter how small, to help their family appreciate and participate in the life of the Church can make a huge difference in the long run.

A young person's family shouldn't be an afterthought in ministry with them, but central to it. Families can be radically different from one another, even in the same neighborhood or parish. Some might be living with a mom and dad. Others might be from a single parent household, a multi-generational home, or foster care. Some might be separated by incarceration, immigration issues, military service, or other factors. Never assume that you understand a teenager's family situation without talking and listening to him or her.

Families of all kinds need the help of the whole Faith community, and our ministry with teens should be intentional in partnering with them to help their young people become disciples of Jesus Christ. This is not an attempt to "replace" the family's role as the primary catechist. Like young people, families also need to be accompanied in their journey of faith as they seek to live out the vocation that God has given them. Many teenagers, transformed by an encounter with Jesus Christ, have awakened the faith of their families.

LIKE YOUNG PEOPLE, FAMILIES ALSO NEED TO BE ACCOMPANIED IN THEIR JOURNEY OF FAITH AS THEY SEEK TO LIVE OUT THE VOCATION THAT GOD HAS GIVEN THEM.

Think of every "information" moment with families as a ministry moment. When I talked to families, I tried to "ricochet" the Gospel to them. I didn't preach to them directly — why would they care what I have to say? Instead, I shared with them what their teens had been learning and doing in the ministries that we provided. For example, if we were just back from a retreat, I gave a highlight talk that included all the major points we covered (a.k.a., the kerygma). I know many in youth ministry who send emails for each youth night that summarizes the message and offers a few questions that parents can ask their teens after the meeting. Some will read it, some won't. You can't control their responses, but you can control your actions. Keep inviting, encouraging, communicating. Do all that you can to keep families involved and empower them to be an active part of the ministry. Some of my most memorable ministry moments occurred when I had the chance to help a family better communicate with each other and grow in faith together.

Use Resources, Love Teenagers

When I started youth ministry, I was desperate for good resources and programs that would be engaging to teenagers and faithful to Catholic teaching. Now there is an abundance of them! There is a plethora (yes, I know what that means) of incredible video series, podcasts, and books that teens can watch, listen to, and read to grow deeper in their faith. There are a number of exceptional programs that provide content for weekly meetings, retreats, or sacramental preparation. It is no longer a question of "Where can I find something good?" but "Which one should I choose?" Do yourself and your teens a favor by familiarizing yourself with all the products and programs that are available — there is always something new! Since you know the teens you minister with, you can find the material that will be most effective for them.

Good ministry programs are an effective way of meeting teenagers and building relationships with them. Though you can't schedule relationships like you do programs, it is still important to have relational goals. I like to think of teens in four age groups with different program/relational goals for each. Here is an example of how I approached parish youth ministry:

- **Junior high:** For younger adolescents in junior high, I think that it is okay to be "program heavy." This is a great age to build relationships with their families since they are still very dependent upon them. Some "tweens" aren't ready for friendships with adults they aren't related to. The ratio of programs to relationships can be 80/20. If I had a weekly youth group meeting (four times a month) I'd try once a month to connect with a junior high student outside of that (mostly seeing them play a sport, theater production, etc.).

- **High school underclassmen:** The ratio of programs to relationships for high school underclassmen can be more like 60/40: weekly programs with two points of contact outside the church each month. At this stage I'm really trying to create opportunities to get to know them better, especially in the fall of their freshman year. Hopefully by the end of their sophomore year they've been on a few retreats, a summer trip, have actively participated in meetings, and have taken up some leadership responsibilities.
- **High school upperclassmen:** This is where it should shift to being more relational than programmatic; the ratio of programs to relationships for this age group should be more like 40/60 or even 20/80. Though I never promoted it this way, I didn't expect the juniors and seniors who had been involved in the ministry to keep coming to the main weekly youth group (unless they helped lead it) — that was primarily evangelistic in nature. Those upperclassmen who remain, and there are fewer of them than the previous two groups, are ready to go deeper. They thrive in small groups, mentoring, and leadership opportunities.
- **+1:** The real relational test is how you connect with teens who graduate from high school, especially those who go away to college. Psychologists say that for many people, their freshman year of college is the loneliest year of their life, and data shows that this is also the time when many teens who were active in their faith stop going to church. If they can stay active in the Faith their first year of college they

> have a much higher rate of staying active in the Faith for the rest of their life! Have a care package ready to get to them within the first two weeks of school. Try to send something once a month. Be aware of their breaks and do something when they get home. They are no longer minors, so you have more flexibility about where and when you can meet with them, but remember to be prudent and above reproach in whatever you do.

I would never confine a teenager to one of those categories if he or she was ready to go deeper! Those guidelines worked for the ministry that I was in at the time, but that doesn't mean that it works for you or the teens you minister with — I provide it only as an example. Since I was a full-time parish youth minister, part of my job was relational ministry. I didn't expect that my volunteers had as much time to do that as I did, though I would still try to set reasonable goals and empower them to achieve them. For example, I'd ask my volunteers to go to two or three high school events each semester, and then I'd look at the school's calendar and give them options where they could "buddy up" with another volunteer to do so.

You can get a lot of exceptional content through programs, but don't rely on them to do ministry for you. You are more than a Catholic content curator. Avoid showing videos of "talking heads" delivering information — that is such an adult thing to do! I'd rather have a less professional talk given by an adult who is a friend with the teens than a great talk from a stranger. Do you know what? Teenagers would rather have that, too.

When Joel Stepanek (former vice president of Life Teen International) gave a presentation to one of my classes, he said, "We spend a lot of time making quality resources so you can spend more time building quality relationships." Boom. *That* is the best thing about good resources and programs: They allow you to spend less time with planning and more time with people. Never forget that the best "resource" that you have is the Gospel written on your heart.

Questions for Reflection and Discussion

- What are some specific things that you can do to "be a teen" to teenagers? How can you learn more about their cultures?
- How did this chapter change what you thought you knew about accompaniment? Which bullet point (on pages 145–47) was most helpful to you and why?
- Are you familiar with the safe environment policies of your diocese? What are some ways that the ministry you are involved with can create "places of accompaniment" that are both safe and relational? How could you connect with teenagers outside church property or scheduled meetings (N.B.: This might be a question that someone in the diocese can answer†)?
- How might you more effectively partner with families?
- What specific relational goals can you set for the ministry that you are involved in?

† If the answer is "Never," then I'd encourage more conversation about that. At the very least, one should be allowed to attend public events (sports, concerts, plays) that teens are a part of. Can you go with a bunch of teens to Dairy Queen afterward? Can you have dinner and then a meeting with upperclassmen who are helping to plan a retreat at your house if there are other adults present? Could you do that at one of the teen's houses? The more you are connecting with teenagers at unscheduled moments and off church property, the more relational the ministry naturally becomes (because this is how their other relationships work). The goal is not to find "loopholes," however, but to be transparent and obedient.

12
Joyful Young Disciples

What is our goal of doing ministry with youths? This is an important question. Goals that aren't frequently articulated are rarely (if ever) achieved. Is it to keep kids out of trouble? To keep cultural traditions alive? Is it to educate them about the Faith? Or get more young people involved in service?

All of the above are good. But the ultimate goal of ministry, with youths or anyone, is to help people become the saints God has created them to be. Too lofty? Michelangelo once said, "The great danger for most of us lies not in setting our aim too high and falling short; but in setting our aim too low, and achieving our mark." I also like this quote from Les Brown: "Shoot for the moon. Even if you miss, you'll land among the stars."

When we hear the word *saints* we think of images enshrined in stained glass of holy men and women who have gone to heaven. However, Saint Paul often used the words *saints* or *holy ones* to address those still on earth, men and women who had been sanctified by Jesus Christ and were striving to do his will, even if they struggled at times to do it. Another word that the Bible uses to describe that kind of person is *disciple*.

Though *Listen, Teach, Send* is the most recent framework for ministries with youths and young adults, I believe that there is still some value in looking at the previous framework that the US bishops created that was specific to teenagers, *Renewing the Vision*. It said that the primary goal of ministry with adolescents was "to empower young people to live as disciples of Jesus Christ in our world today." Moreover:

> The challenge of discipleship — of following Jesus — is at the heart of the Church's mission. All ministry with adolescents must be directed toward presenting young people with the Good News of Jesus Christ and inviting and challenging them to become his disciples. ... We are confident that young people will commit themselves totally to Jesus Christ, who will ask everything from them and give everything in return. We need to provide concrete ways by which the demands, excitement, and adventure of being a disciple of Jesus Christ can be personally experienced by adolescents — where they tax and test their resources and where they stretch their present capacities and skills to the limits. ... Growth in discipleship is not about offering a particular program; it is the goal of all our efforts.

As mentioned earlier, *youth ministry* is a broad and general term that can cover a wide array of ministries. Depending on that ministry, more specific goals can be included. For example, a Catholic ministry for teenage girls who are pregnant would include goals of helping ensure a healthy and safe delivery, providing necessary training and materials for the mother, helping the baby get adopted (if that is what the mother wants), and so forth. Those goals would differ from a confirmation preparation program, where the goals would include an understanding of the rite, a catechesis on confirmation, opportunities for service, and so forth.

REGARDLESS OF THE MINISTRY CONTEXT, THE GOAL OF INVITING AND EMPOWERING TEENAGERS TO BE DISCIPLES OF JESUS IS ALWAYS AT THE HEART OF EVERY MINISTRY WITH TEENS.

Regardless of the ministry context, the goal of inviting and empowering teenagers to be disciples of Jesus is always at the heart of every ministry with teens. They need to know that Jesus is the one who "is living at your side every day to enlighten, strengthen and free you" (*Evangelii Gaudium*, 164). Every ministry should ask, "How are we modeling discipleship for these adolescents? How are we inviting and empowering them to be like Jesus? What are we doing to help them hear his call?" Part of that answer has been the theme of this book. To go the second mile. Build relationships outside the programs that lead them to Jesus. Share the faith through friendship.

In addition to emphasizing the essential goal of discipleship, another fruit of *Renewing the Vision* was explaining different components of ministry with adolescents that should also be a part of those ministries. Over the past few decades, many in youth ministry have found this to be tremendously helpful so that their ministry with teens might not be one-dimensional but comprehensive. To state the obvious, a lot has occurred in the Church and the world over the past twenty-five years since that document was written! Though its concepts still ring true, some of its language is outdated.

GROWTH
VOCATIONAL
COMMUNAL
SACRAMENTAL
THE YOUNG JESUS
MISSIONARY
OUTREACH
CATECHETICAL
HUMANITARIAN
KERYGMATIC
ACCOMPANIMENT
CATHOLIC CHURCH

A Eucharistic Analogy

I'd like to conclude this book by re-articulating the components of youth ministry in *Renewing the Vision*, using terminology more fitting for today (especially with language used by Pope Francis). Much of this summarizes what was said before, but I hope that it helps to visualize how relational and incarnational ministry fits into the bigger picture of all ministries with youths. Since so many Catholic teenagers have had profound conversion moments during Eucharistic adoration, I thought that I might use that image as an analogy for how a relational approach to Catholic youth ministry fits within the bigger picture.

Though there can be many things that enhance Eucharistic adoration — music, incense, preaching, and the like — three things that are essential are an altar, a monstrance, and, of course, the Eucharist. In this analogy for Catholic youth ministry, the altar is the Church. She is the means by which Christ becomes present to us. The monstrance is the ministry of accompaniment. And the Eucharist itself is the young Jesus, who is the heart of youth ministry.

The Catholic Church

> Then Jesus approached and said to them, "All power in heaven and on earth has been given to me. Go, therefore, and make disciples of all nations, baptizing them in the name of the Father, and of the Son, and of the holy Spirit, teaching them to observe all that I have commanded you. And behold, I am with you always, until the end of the age." (Matthew 28:18–20)

Jesus instituted the Church as a means by which we can hear his voice and draw closer to his heart. She is both Christ's Body and his Bride. No one can be connected to the head without being a part of the body; no one can be wed to the groom without being part of the bride. Christ entrusted to her the saving message which we are to share with the world. All ministry with youths is part of the Church's ministry of evangelization.

Young people are not the future of the Church, they are its present! The Church desperately needs the young to "renew her spiritual ardor and her apostolic vigor. The balm of holiness generated by the good lives of so many young people can heal the wounds of the Church and of the world, bringing us back to that fullness of love to which we have always been called" (*Christus Vivit*, 50).

Accompaniment

> And it happened that while they were conversing and debating, Jesus himself drew near and walked with them. (Luke 24:15)

Where does relational ministry fit in this analogy? The ministry of accompaniment is the monstrance itself. In Latin, the word *monstrance* means "to show." Relational ministry is the way that we show Jesus to teens. If a monstrance is small, Jesus becomes less visible. If a monstrance is ugly, it detracts from the beauty of the Eucharist. If the monstrance is empty, it has no point to it! The same can be said of our relational ministry with teenagers.

Moreover, if there is a Eucharistic procession, the monstrance is the means by which the Real Presence of Jesus leaves the sanctuary, moves among the congregation, and even goes out into the streets. Youth ministry needs accompaniment like the Eucharist needs a monstrance. It is the only way "to show" Christ and to have him process into the world.

The Young Jesus

> Each year his parents went to Jerusalem for the feast of Passover, and when he was twelve years old, they went up according to festival custom. After they had completed its days, as they were returning, the boy Jesus remained behind in Jerusalem, but his parents did not know it. (Luke 2:41–43)

YOUTH MINISTRY NEEDS ACCOMPANIMENT LIKE THE EUCHARIST NEEDS A MONSTRANCE.

The Eucharist is Jesus. In this analogy of youth ministry, we are considering him specifically as "the boy Jesus" (Lk 2:43), the adolescent eager to ask questions, the one who "advanced [in] wisdom and age and favor before God and man" (Lk 2:52). The youthfulness of Jesus is not merely something that he was, but something that he *is*. Saint Irenaeus wrote that Jesus is "young among the young in order to be an example for the young and to consecrate them to the Lord." The Greek word for *new* can also be translated as "young." So, when Saint Paul writes, "So whoever is in Christ is a new creation," that can also mean a "*young* creation." And the words of Jesus in the Book of Revelation can be understood as "Behold, I make all things *young*" (Rv 21:5).

The youth of Jesus has sanctified youth. It is a sacred time and needs not be rushed or looked down upon as if there was something wrong with it. Though we want to guide adolescents into maturity, our goal is not to make them act older than they are, but to help them celebrate their faith in a way proper to the sacred age that they are in. Young people can be louder, more emotional, and messier than older generations. This should be embraced! Overly serious ministries with young people can fall into the trap of making an evangelizer look like "someone who has just come back from a funeral" (*Evangelii Gaudium*, 10).

Pope Francis understood the importance of being youthful when he told young people to "Make a ruckus!" (*Christus Vivit*, 143). The zeal, energy, joy, and even silliness that young people express is something that the Church would benefit from. "Christian joy is usually accompanied by a sense of humor. ... Ill humor is no sign of holiness" (*Gaudate et Exsultate*, 126). Unfortunately, the experience of many young people in the Church feels "like Lent without Easter" (*Evangelii Gaudium*, 6).

The boy Jesus is at the heart of all ministries with youths. He comes to them as they are, not as we are. As Catholics, we are not called to be members of an organization, but joyful missionary disciples of *him*. He is alive! We share this truth by witnessing to how Christ is alive in us, showing teenagers how Christ is alive in them. All these components of ministry with youths must reflect the youthfulness of Jesus and the youthfulness of the ones we do ministry with, inviting them to "shout with joy to the LORD, all the earth; / break into song; sing praise" (Ps 98:4) because "God loves the joy of young people" (*Christus Vivit*, 167). He is the "young among the young."

The Components of Youth Ministry

Surrounding the Eucharist on the face of the monstrance in the image are seven components, all connecting back to the young Jesus. These components are Communal, Missionary, Humanitarian, Kerygmatic, Catechetical, Sacramental, and Vocational. It is important to recognize that, though different ministries with teenagers might emphasize one component more than another, they all should challenge themselves to incorporate each of these components into their ministry with youths, or collaborate with other ministries that can. We will look at each of these components in detail in a moment.

First, notice that around those components on the face of the monstrance are two arrows that point clockwise, highlighting the two movements of ministry: outreach and growth. Pope Francis wrote, "I wish simply to emphasize that youth ministry involves two main courses of action. One is *outreach*, the way we attract new young people to an experience of the Lord. The other is *growth*, the way we help those who have already had that experience to mature in it" (*Christus Vivit*, 209). The components focused on *outreach* are Communal, Missionary, Humanitarian, and Kerygmatic. The components of *growth* are Kerygmatic, Catechetical, Sacramental, Vocational, and Communal.

You probably noticed some repetition there! That is intentional. The components that overlap are Communal and Kerygmatic. This is because ministry flows out of and back to the community, and ministry leads to and grows from the kerygma. I have categorized these seven components based on who the action is toward, not the one who performs it, since any outreach to another is an opportunity of growth for the one who is doing it.

Communal

> Every day they devoted themselves to meeting together in the temple area and to breaking bread in their homes. They ate their meals with exultation and sincerity of heart, praising God and enjoying favor with all the people. And every day the Lord added to their number those who were being saved. (Acts of the Apostles 2:46–47)

Discipleship is not lived in isolation but in the context of a community of faith. This begins in the family. "The family is the central place where the community of life and love are celebrated. Therefore, the Church's ministry with adolescents should lead young people into a deeper faith life within their own families" (*Renewing the Vision*). It is essential to incorporate the families of teenagers in our ministry with them as best we can.

"Youth ministry is the response of the Christian community to the needs of young people, and the sharing of the unique gifts of youth with the larger community" (*A Vision of Youth Ministry*). Those who do ministry with youths need to be advocates for them to the wider faith community, and the community is responsible to provide what resources it can to help as many teenagers as possible. Young people need to be welcomed into the parish community as active participants, who have gifts to share and ideas worth listening to. "Certainly they need to he [*sic*] helped and guided, but at the same time left free to develop new approaches, with creativity and a certain audacity" (*Christus Vivit*, 203). Youth ministers should not only see their mission as accompanying the young, but also to do what they can to empower the faith community to do ministry with teens.

YOUTH MINISTERS SHOULD NOT ONLY SEE THEIR MISSION AS ACCOMPANYING THE YOUNG, BUT ALSO TO DO WHAT THEY CAN TO EMPOWER THE FAITH COMMUNITY TO DO MINISTRY WITH TEENS.

In addition to helping build community among their peers, ministries with young people should foster intergenerational and intercultural relationships that introduce them into the wider family of the Catholic Faith. This also includes the communion of saints, a heritage of faith that not only provides inspirational stories of the past but living intercessors in the present: "May we also be their companions and fellow disciples!" (CCC 957).

We must also build bridges to ecumenical ministries so that teenagers can recognize peers and adults from different Christian faith traditions as fellow disciples of Jesus Christ who share in the same baptismal grace. Protestant scholar Glen Scorgie wryly noted that, "The Holy Spirit seems to be far less discerning with who he hangs out with than we are." There is more that unites us than divides. Catholic and Protestant teenagers have many challenges in common: finding time to pray, standing up for their values in public, living chaste relationships, and witnessing their Faith to others. Catholics and Protestants in ministry together is a powerful witness of Faith and answers the prayer of Jesus at the Last Supper, "I pray not only for them [the apostles], but also for those who will believe in me through their word, so that they may all be one" (Jn 17:20–21). Positive relationships with open-minded Protestant peers can give a Catholic teenager an opportunity to learn how to articulate the specifics of their Catholic Faith in a way that they may not have otherwise — an important skill for college and for life!

Missionary

> But you will receive power when the holy Spirit comes upon you, and you will be my witnesses in Jerusalem, throughout Judea and Samaria, and to the ends of the earth. (Acts of the Apostles 1:8)

"If we can hear what the Spirit is saying to us, we have to realize that youth [and young adult] ministry is always missionary" (*Christus Vivit*, 240). Jesus told his apostles to "Go, therefore, and make disciples of all nations" (Mt 28:19), not "Stay, and expect everyone to come to you." Ministry that leads people to Jesus should reflect the Incarnation, the Word-made-Flesh that dwells among his people.

"The pilgrim Church is missionary by her very nature" (*Ad Gentes*, 2) She seeks to learn about and engage the cultures of those to whom she ministers, and burns with the heart of Jesus to "seek and to save what was lost" (Lk 19:10). As such, effective ministry cannot happen behind a desk or be successfully promoted in a Church bulletin. We must "go" to where the young are, both in what we say (speaking a language that they can understand), and what we do (going to their schools, their places of work and play, etc.).

As a young person answers the call of Jesus, he or she must understand that "Every Christian is a missionary to the extent that he or she has encountered the love of God in Christ Jesus: we no longer say that we are 'disciples' and 'missionaries', but rather that we are always 'missionary disciples'" (*Evangelii Gaudium*, 120). Ministries with youths must encourage young people to have a missionary attitude, not just when on a mission trip, but in all the interactions of their lives. As Pope Francis explains: "It doesn't take much to make young people missionaries. Even those who are most frail, limited and troubled can be missionaries in their own way, for goodness can always be shared, even if it exists alongside many limitations. A young person who makes a pilgrimage to ask Our Lady for help, and invites a friend or companion along, by that single gesture is being a good missionary" (*Christus Vivit*, 239).

Humanitarian

> Then the king will say to those on his right, "Come, you who are blessed by my Father. Inherit the kingdom prepared for you from the foundation of the world. For I

> was hungry and you gave me food, I was thirsty and you gave me drink, a stranger and you welcomed me, naked and you clothed me, ill and you cared for me, in prison and you visited me." (Matthew 25:34–36)

"The situation often demands that the apostolate amongst young people be an animation of a *missionary or humanitarian nature*, as a necessary first step to bringing to maturity those dispositions favorable to the strictly catechetical moment" (*General Directory for Catechesis*, 185). Nearly one in two children will see their parent's marriage break up (and those children are twice as likely to drop out of high school). One in nine women will experience some form of sexual assault. One out of five youths and young adults say that they have seriously considered suicide, and nearly one out of ten have attempted it. These are just some of the startling statistics about young people in the United States.

Pope Francis said, "I see the church as a field hospital after battle. It is useless to ask a seriously injured person if he has high cholesterol and about the level of his blood sugars! You have to heal his wounds. Then we can talk about everything else." Ministry with adolescents must assist the natural well-being of young people before it can address the supernatural. Pastoral leaders must advocate for young people on the margins and in crisis situations. If ministries are not equipped to help young people in those situations, they should connect the young with those who can.

Some of the biggest crises with youths are psychological. Sometimes a teenager simply needs a mature friend who can listen and encourage them, a "nonjudgmental validating presence." Others require professional help. Dr. Kristin Witte, the former director of pastoral care for the Archdiocese of Baltimore, suggested that youth ministry should be "triage" in those situations: Try to stop the bleeding, then get them to the help that they need. Obviously, the family should be involved — they know their teen better than you do. All ministries with youths should be familiar with counseling services (especially Catholic ones) that can bring healing to young people and their families while still accompanying them on the path of friendship (not just passing them off).

The humanitarian component is not only *to* young people in need, but *with* young people as they become disciples of Jesus. "Social engagement and direct contact with the poor remain fundamental ways of finding or deepening one's faith and the discernment of one's vocation" (*Christus Vivit*, 170). Young people need to know that the best way to show their love for Jesus is not just by time in prayer, but also in service to the poor and those in who are need: "Amen, I say to you, whatever you did for one of these least brothers of mine, you did for me" (Mt 25:40).

Kerygmatic

> But when the fullness of time had come, God sent his Son, born of a woman, born under the law, to ransom those under the law, so that we might receive adoption. As proof that you are children, God sent the spirit of his Son into our hearts, crying out, "Abba, Father!" So you are no longer a slave but a child, and if a child then also an heir, through God. (Galatians 4:4–7)

"All Christian formation consists of entering more deeply into the kerygma" (*Evangelii Gaudium*, 165). This is not the mere recitation of a formula, but a process by which one, through experience and explanation, can understand the love of God as shown through Jesus Christ.

Teenagers must first *see* the Gospel in our lives before they can be open to hearing it. "The Good News proclaimed by the witness of life sooner or later has to be proclaimed by the word of life. There is no true evangelization if the name, the teaching, the life, the promises, the kingdom and the mystery of Jesus of Nazareth, the Son of God are not proclaimed" (*Evangelii Nuntiandi*, 22). Young people need to hear a clear proclamation of Jesus Christ and the story of salvation. They must understand the devastating effects of sin so that they can more deeply embrace and experience God's mercy, for "God proves his love for us in that while we were still sinners Christ died for us" (Rom 5:8) and "now there is no condemnation for those who are in Christ Jesus" (Rom 8:1).

Ministries with teenagers must do more than proclaim the kerygma once and move on to other things. They must be constantly kerygmatic:

> It would be a serious mistake to think that in youth ministry "the kerygma should give way to a supposedly more 'solid' formation. Nothing is more solid, profound, secure, meaningful and wisdom-filled than that initial proclamation. All Christian formation consists of entering more deeply into the kerygma" and incarnating it ever more fully in our lives. Consequently, youth ministry should always include occasions for renewing and deepening our personal experience of the love of God and the living Christ. It can do this in a variety of ways: testimonies, songs, moments of adoration, times of spiritual reflection on the sacred Scriptures, and even an intelligent use of social networks (*Christus Vivit,* 214).

Understanding this Good News not only draws one closer to God but also to others. "The kerygma has a clear social content: at the very heart of the Gospel is life in community and engagement with others. The content of the first proclamation has an immediate moral implication centered on charity" (*Evangelii Gaudium*, 177).

Catechetical

> Those who accepted his message were baptized, and about three thousand persons were added that day. They devoted themselves to the teaching of the apostles and to the communal life, to the breaking of the bread and to the prayers. (Acts of the Apostles 2:41–42)

"Quite early on, the name *catechesis* was given to the totality of the Church's efforts to make disciples, to help men believe that Jesus is the Son of God so that believing they might have life in his name, and to educate and instruct them in this life, thus building up the body of Christ" (CCC 4). Catechesis trains one for the life of discipleship, the aim of which is "to put people not only in touch but in communion, in intimacy, with Jesus Christ: only He can lead us to the love of the Father in the Spirit and make us share in the life of the Holy Trinity" (*Catechesi Tradendae*, 5).

Though education and a systematic presentation of the Faith are important parts of this component, it must not be limited to a purely academic experience. The knowledge imparted in catechesis is given to help one fall more deeply in love with Jesus, unpacking the beauty of the kerygma. At times, the truths revealed by God are contrary to the cultures in which young people live, and they need to be explained "with gentleness and reverence" (1 Pt 3:16).

THE KNOWLEDGE IMPARTED IN CATECHESIS IS GIVEN TO HELP ONE FALL MORE DEEPLY IN LOVE WITH JESUS, UNPACKING THE BEAUTY OF THE KERYGMA.

Young people have the right to hear a comprehensive and systematic presentation of the Faith (Creed, sacraments, morality, prayer), not just occasional topics given in an improvised fashion. The goal is not *convincing* but *conversion*, which is a work of the Holy Spirit. "For adherence on the part of those to be taught is a fruit of grace and freedom, and does not ultimately depend on the catechist; and catechetical action, therefore, should be accompanied by prayer" (*General Catechetical Directory*, 71).

Sacramental

> But when they came to Jesus and saw that he was already dead, they did not break his legs, but one soldier thrust his lance into his side, and immediately blood and water flowed out. (John 19:33–34)

Ministries with adolescents must invite young people into sacramental celebrations and help them understand the presence of Christ within them. They must learn that baptism, confirmation, and Eucharist "lay the *foundations* of every Christian life" (CCC 1212); how Jesus continues the work of "healing and salvation" (1421) in the Sacraments of Reconciliation and Anointing of the Sick; and how the graces of holy orders and matrimony "are directed towards the salvation of others" (1534). Just as Jesus accomplished his saving work through the suffering, death, resurrection, and ascension of his physical body, he continues to dispense his powers in physical ways.

"The mysteries of Christ's life are the foundations of what he would henceforth dispense in the sacraments" (1115). One need not feel a loss that they did not live two thousand years ago to have a physical encounter with Jesus. That is what occurs in the sacraments! "Sacraments are 'powers that comes [*sic*] forth' from the Body of Christ, which is ever-living and life-giving. They are actions of the Holy Spirit at work in his Body, the Church" (1116).

Through the witness and invitation of other joyful disciples, young people can enter into a full, active, and conscious participation in the Mass. Pope St. Paul VI wrote, "The role of evangelization is precisely to educate people in the faith in such a way as to lead each individual Christian to live the sacraments as true sacraments of faith — and not to receive them passively or reluctantly" (*Evangelii Nuntiandi*, 47). This is especially important considering the many transitions that adolescents face, especially for those who go away to college. Wherever they are, Jesus is present for them in the sacraments, most especially in the Eucharist, "the sum and summary of our faith" (CCC 1327).

Catechetical formation is necessary for vibrant sacramental celebration and vice versa. "Sacramental life is impoverished and very soon turns into hollow ritualism if it is not based on serious knowledge of the meaning of the sacraments, and catechesis becomes intellectualized if it fails to come alive in the sacramental practice" (*Catechesi Tradendae*, 23).

Vocational

> Then I heard the voice of the Lord saying, "Whom shall I send? Who will go for us?" "Here I am," I said; "send me!" (Isaiah 6:8)

Helping young people discern their mission, their vocation, is at the heart of ministries with teenagers. Thus, the Final Document for the Synod on "Young People, the Faith, and Vocational Discernment" stated:

> From the beginning of the synodal process, it became very clear that youth ministry needs a vocational slant. In this way, the two essential characteristics of a pastoral approach to young generations emerge: it is "for youth,"

> because it is aimed at those in the singular and unrepeatable stage in life which is youth; it is "vocational," because youth is the privileged season for life choices and for responding to God's call. The "vocationality" of youth ministry should not be understood in an exclusive sense, but an intensive sense. God calls at every age in life — from the mother's womb to old age — but youth is the privileged moment for listening, for availability and for accepting God's will.

Many teens think that vocations are something to consider for the future, such as discernment of marriage, single life, religious life, or ordained ministry. However, our first vocation is a friendship with Jesus. That is something to be lived here and now, and from that other vocations emerge. Ministries with teenagers are not only about helping young people hear the voice of God but also helping them learn how to speak the voice that God gave them into the world. In *Christus Vivit*, Francis drew attention to other kinds of vocations, such as art, music, or sport. Every young person needs to hear:

OUR FIRST VOCATION IS A FRIENDSHIP WITH JESUS.

> In discerning your vocation, it is important to determine if you see in yourself the abilities needed to perform that specific service to society.
>
> This gives greater value to everything you do. Your work stops being just about making money, keeping busy or pleasing others. It becomes your vocation because you are called to it; it is something more than merely a pragmatic decision. In the end, it is a recognition of why

> I was made, why I am here on earth, and what the Lord's plan is for my life. (*Christus Vivit*, 255–256)

Young people need to know that the vocations to which they are called are not opposed to the desires of their heart, but their fulfillment, even if they may not appear so at first. "For I know well the plans I have in mind for you … plans for your welfare and not for woe, so as to give you a future of hope" (Jer 29:11). They can learn this through the loving accompaniment of men and women who, following the prompting of the Spirit in their own lives, have found a peace and joy in answering the call of Jesus that the world cannot give.

Into the Harvest!

For me, learning to do ministry with young people was similar to learning to play guitar. My fingers hurt at first until I got used to it. I learned a few chords so that I could play a few songs. Every new chord added another group of songs that I could play. I didn't sound good at first. Then it became passable. Then it became enjoyable! As the saying goes, "You have to walk before you can run."

It is the same with doing ministry with teenagers. Be patient with yourself. You are bound to have some awkward moments. You'll get confused looks from teens as they try to figure you out. You'll invest a lot of time with no visible results. You'll begin to wonder why nothing is happening. And then — something will. A genuine conversation. A moment of vulnerability. An opportunity to serve. A movement of the Spirit.

The ministry that we do with young people as teenagers is a small part of their lives, but it is an important part. It takes time to see the fruit. When I worked at a parish, I asked the volunteers who did ministry with me to try to commit for at least three years. It takes about that long to be trusted and welcomed into a community of teenagers who are accustomed to adults coming and going. Ministry that is relational and incarnational is a marathon, not a sprint. The Word did not become flesh for a quick visit, but to pitch his tent among us and stay for a while. The greatest ability that we can share with teenagers is availability.

There is always more to learn about ministry with youths. Each of those components could be its own book! But none of those components will be effective if our ministry with teenagers isn't grounded in holy friendships. Discipleship needs to be modeled, and it is most clearly evident in the "second mile." The Gospel needs to be seen before it is heard, read on the hearts of believers who are willing to leave their comfort zones and dwell among the young. Teenagers need to read many of these "letters of Christ" before they can be convinced of the truth and beauty of the Good News. *You* are one of those important pages. So *go* and open your heart to them!

THE GREATEST ABILITY THAT WE CAN SHARE WITH TEENAGERS IS AVAILABILITY.

"The harvest is abundant but the laborers are few; so ask the master of the harvest to send out laborers for his harvest" (Mt 9:37–38). Let us offer this prayer on our knees and answer it with our hands and feet. Let us ask for grace-filled opportunities to accompany teenagers though the many challenges and transitions that they face. Let us be open to allow the Spirit to speak through us and listen to the Spirit speak through the young, so that together we can share the Faith through friendships, sharing the Gospel with our lives.

Questions for Reflection and Discussion

- This is the end of the book, so it is time to get specific and practical. How does the ministry that you do with teenagers (and/or the ministry that you are involved with) empower them to be joyful disciples of Jesus in our world today?
- What are the other tangible goals of your ministry with youths?
- When you look at these components of ministry, which ones does your ministry do best? What can be done about those components that are either not done or done poorly?
- Now that you are done with the book, how did this book help you understand relational ministry in new ways, and what ideas are you the most excited to implement in your ministry with adolescents?

A Final Exercise

Go back and examine your answers to the questions posed at the end of each chapter of this book. They can be organized into four categories: Jesus, you, teenagers, and ministry. Use the below question prompts to highlight what you learned in each category. The "ministry" category is best answered within a group.

- **Jesus:** What did you learn about him? How do you see him differently? What did you learn from him? How can you proclaim him (the kerygma)?
- **You:** Is your identity based on being a son or daughter of God? How can you grow in your prayer life? How did the Scriptures inspire you? What are your motivations for ministry with teens?
- **Teens:** What are their felt needs? Where are their "wells"? How do you understand them differently after reading this book? How might you accompany them?

- **Ministry:** What are the goals of the ministry with teens you are involved with? How can programs within that ministry be more relational? Which components are in most need of attention? What goals can be set to connect with teenagers outside those programs?

Appendix
Further Study

You want to read *more*? Okay, now I feel bad about that "reader" comment I made in the first chapter. Clearly, it doesn't apply to you!

The first thing you should read are the Gospels. I mean it. *Read* the Gospels. I loved this line from *Listen, Teach, Send*: "The Gospels have a 'special preeminence' among all the Scriptures, since 'they are the principal witness of the life and teaching of the Incarnate Word, our Savior' (CCC, 81). The Gospels should likewise be preeminent in the lives of all missionary disciples." Don't get me wrong, I love audiobooks and podcasts. But listening to a recording of the Gospel while you are brushing your teeth or going for a run is no substitute for sitting down and reading through the Gospels one page at a time. There are no better books about Jesus that have ever been written!

Then you should read the *Catechism of the Catholic Church*. I know, it is a big book. Start with the fourth section on prayer. It is beautiful and will change the way you pray! Then I'd go to the beginning and prayerfully reflect on one "In Brief" every day. If you read something you don't understand or are curious about, you can go back into that section and learn more about it. Eventually you should read the whole Bible and *Catechism*, but the Gospels, the *Catechism*'s section on prayer, and the "In Brief" conclusions to the other sections are a great place to start.

If it wasn't obvious from the abundance of quotes I included throughout this book, Pope Francis's *Christus Vivit* is a must read for anyone doing ministry with young people. Be aware that Francis's definition of *young people* and *youth ministry* is different than what we commonly mean in the United States. He is referring to people between the ages of sixteen and thirty. Using our terminology, it might be more accurate to call it a "young adult" document, but almost all the principles apply to ministry with teenagers. I'd also recommend his first encyclical, *Evangelii Gaudium* (The Joy of the Gospel). What Francis proposed in this encyclical he has implemented in *Christus Vivit.*

Listen, Teach, Send: National Pastoral Framework for Ministries with Youth and Young Adults by the USCCB would be next. It was ambitious to create one document for both youth ministry and young adult ministry (they previously had their own frameworks). One downside of addressing a group that large and diverse is a lack of specificity for those respective fields. I hope this book has filled in some of those gaps for youth ministry. For extra credit, look at the previous framework, *Renewing the Vision.* As I said earlier, some of the language doesn't hold up, but the general concepts still apply.

Though I don't have additional titles to recommend, don't be afraid to read a book by a Protestant author — many Protestant youth ministries are exceptional at relational ministry, and you can easily "translate" those ideas into a Catholic context. Secular books can be helpful as well. I've gotten a lot of great insights from books on business leadership, marketing, and youth culture. Whatever you do, *keep reading and learning.* Anything that can help you be more effective in sharing the Gospel with teenagers is worth it.

Finally, I've helped create many youth ministry training videos that are available through the Catechetical Institute at Franciscan University (franciscanathome.com). Over half of the dioceses in the United States use these as formation for their youth ministers and catechists. You may find these videos useful for your ministry as well.

Acknowledgments

My family is awesome. I'd like to thank to my wife, Jennifer, and my seven kids, who let me hide in my office for hours on end to write this book.

I would not have been able to finish it were it not for the support of my colleagues at Franciscan University of Steubenville, especially Eric Westby, James Pauley, Scott Sollom, and Ron Bolster. I am indebted to my mentor Barbara Morgan, who challenged me to take my studies seriously, and I certainly wouldn't be teaching at Franciscan were it not for her advocacy and support. Thanks to those in the administration (especially Daniel Kempton and Steve Hildebrand), who granted me some time off to write.

Much of what I've reflected in this book I've learned from some of the best voices in Catholic youth ministry, especially those who have been kind enough to lecture to my students (while I was taking copious notes in the back): Jim Beckman, Karen Reynolds, Joel Stepanek, Kristin Witte, Josh Miller, Anna Carter, Gina Bauer, and Diana Hancharenko. Some of this content also came from my Ph.D. dissertation that I would not have gotten through were it not for the kindness and patience of my wonderful supervisor, Andrew Morris.

I sent an early draft of this book to trusted friends and colleagues. Their feedback and encouragement made this book better than anything I could have written on my own! In addition to those I've already mentioned, I'd like to thank Tom Acemoglu, Tom East, Christine Najarian, Nic Frank, Lauren Wright, Michael Havercamp, Oscar Rivera, and Tom Neal.

A special thanks to Young Life. As a teen I got to experience relational ministry from them firsthand. After college I spent a couple of years being trained on Young Life staff. Now I get to work with them through their office of "Catholic Relations." Luis and Jill Cataldo were my youth ministers as a teen; Tom Hammond was my "trainer" as an adult (and I likely stole more from him than I know).

I am so grateful for the relationship I've had with Life Teen over my decades of ministry, first as a parish youth minister, then as an area director, now as a colleague who occasionally gets to present at their conferences. Life Teen provides amazing training and resources for those in Catholic youth ministry, and I can't recommend them highly enough. Thanks to Randy Raus for his support and encouragement to me over the years. A very big "thank you" goes to Mark Hart, my brother in Christ and in ministry, who was kind enough to write the foreword for this book.

Finally, I'd like to thank Paul Jarzembowski. He was just starting his job at the USCCB when I was starting my dissertation. His help, both then and now, has been invaluable for me to see Catholic youth ministry from a broader, national perspective, and a number of things in this book were inspired from our many conversations about ministry with youths.

Sources

XV Ordinary Synod of Bishops. *Young People, the Faith, and Vocational Discernment.* October 27, 2018. Final Document. Vatican.va.

Benedict XVI. Address to German Pilgrims. April 25, 2005. Vatican.va.

——. Homily. February 19, 2012. Vatican.va.

Congregation for the Clergy. *General Directory for Catechesis.* United States Conference of Catholic Bishops, 1998.

Francis. *Christus Vi-vit.* March 25, 2019. Vatican.va.

——. *Evangelii Gaudium.* November 24, 2013. Vatican.va.

Groeschel, Benedict. *Spiritual Passages: The Psychology of Spiritual Development.* New York: Crossroad, 1983.

John Paul II. Address at 15th World Youth Day Vigil of Prayer. August 19, 2000. Vatican.va.

——. *Catechesi Tradendae.* October 16, 1979. Vatican.va.

——. *Novo Millennio Ineunte.* January 6, 2001. Vatican.va.

——I. *Redemptoris Missio.* December 7, 1990. Vatican.va.

Mercandante, Frank. *Engaging a New Generation: A Vision for*

Reaching Catholic Teens. Huntington, IN: Our Sunday Visitor, 2012.

Paul VI. *Evangelii Nuntiandi*. December 8, 1975. Vatican.va.

Second Vatican Council. *Ad Gentes*. December 7, 1965. Vatican.va.

Sheen, Fulton J. *Life of Christ*. New York: McGraw Hill, 1958.

———. "The Woman at the Well." *The Catholic Hour*. 1952.

Smith, Christian. *Soul Searching: The Religious and Spiritual Lives of American Teenagers*. New York: Oxford University Press, 2005.

USCCB. *A Vision of Youth Ministry*. 1976.

———. *Listen, Teach, Send: A National Pastoral Framework for Ministries with Youth and Young Adults*. 2024.

About the Author

Bob Rice loves being Catholic. He is a husband, father of seven, permanent deacon for the Diocese of Steubenville, and professor of catechetics at Franciscan University of Steubenville. He has a Ph.D. in Theology from Liverpool Hope University, where he researched Catholic youths and evangelization. Deacon Bob is a highly sought-after presenter at parish and diocesan conferences, especially those focused on youths and diaconal ministry. He is the cohost of a popular weekly podcast called *They That Hope* with Fr. Dave Pivonka, TOR. He is also a singer-songwriter whose music can be found on Apple Music, Spotify, and others. Small children trust him, and woodland creatures eat from his hand. He speaks fluent English. You can find out more about him at deaconbobrice.com.